**FIRE's** Guide to
Due Process and Campus Justice

FIRE's *Guides* to Student Rights on Campus

thefire.org/guides

FIRE's *Guide to Free Speech on Campus*

FIRE's *Guide to Due Process and Campus Justice*

FIRE's *Guide to Religious Liberty on Campus*

FIRE's *Guide to Student Fees, Funding, and Legal Equality on Campus*

FIRE's *Guide to First-Year Orientation and Thought Reform on Campus*

FIRE's Guide to
Due Process and Campus Justice

AUTHORS
Harvey A. Silverglate
Josh Gewolb

EDITOR
William Creeley

FOUNDATION FOR INDIVIDUAL RIGHTS IN EDUCATION
Philadelphia

Library of Congress Control Number: 2014957908

ISBN 978-0-9724712-6-8

Published in the United States of America by:
Foundation for Individual Rights in Education
170 S. Independence Mall W., Suite 510
Philadelphia, Pennsylvania 19106

Cover design by Ryan Starr.

Printed in the United States of America.

ACKNOWLEDGMENTS

FIRE's *Guides* to Student Rights on Campus are made possible by contributions from thousands of individual donors and by the support of a number of foundations, including:

The Achelis and Bodman Foundations
Aequus Institute
Anonymous
The Atlas Economic Research Foundation
Earhart Foundation
Pierre F. and Enid Goodrich Foundation
The Joseph Harrison Jackson Foundation
John Templeton Foundation

FIRE gratefully acknowledges their generous support.

If you would like to support FIRE's efforts to promote civil liberties on campus—efforts that include the distribution of this *Guide* to students across the country—please visit thefire.org/donate.

CONTENTS

ix

Contents

Contents

Contents

Contents

PREFACE

The Foundation for Individual Rights in Education (FIRE) is proud to present our *Guide to Due Process and Campus Justice*, an updated edition of our *Guide to Due Process and Fair Procedure on Campus*, published in 2003.

As a student, you should be aware of your right to due process—and how to assert and defend it. Being well informed about your protections from arbitrary and unfair decisionmaking is crucially important, both during your time at college and in the larger world that awaits you beyond campus.

This newly revised *Guide*, the latest in our series of *Guides to Student Rights on Campus*, is intended to provide students with a clear, effective primer on the right to due process. But it is not *only* for students. Faculty, administrators, parents, alumni, friends, citizens, advisors, and attorneys who care about students' rights should understand the threats to due process on campuses nationwide and the means of combating those threats.

FIRE's *Guides* are designed to restore fundamental rights and the values of a free society to our nation's colleges and universities. Our *Guides* also remind those who write, revise, and enforce campus policies of the legal and moral constraints that must guide their authority. The sooner that colleges and universities understand their obligations to a free and decent society, the less need there will be for *Guides* such as these.

PART I: INTRODUCTION

This *Guide* is about what we have come to call "due process"—or, put more simply, fair procedure. Over the course of many centuries, our society has developed a sense of what is proper or indecent, useful or harmful, right or wrong in the treatment of individuals charged with wrongdoing. There were times when there was no presumption of innocence, no reasonable standard of proof, no right to impartial judges, no freedom to defend oneself, and no prohibition against even torture and other processes that are the enemies of both justice and truth. Over time, we have learned that we cannot separate *how* we reach decisions from the justice of those decisions. In other words, the process by which we arrive at a verdict affects how confident we can be in the accuracy of that verdict.

The concepts addressed in this *Guide* may appear technical and dry. That's always a danger when studying the language of lawyers. But the notions of due process, fundamental fairness, and fair procedure are as vital and necessary to society as any area of the law. Indeed, they concern the deepest issues of how we have learned to live together as decent human beings. Think about it: If an innocent person is charged with wrongdoing, what protections should that innocent person have against being wrongly or arbitrarily punished and dishonored? If you or a loved one—your brother, sister, father, mother, or friend—had to face a tribunal and its rules, what expectations of fair procedure and an honest search for truth would you truly have? If you would not want yourself or a loved one tried in unjust ways, how could you morally accept seeing other people tried under those conditions? The issues discussed in this *Guide* touch upon the rules and learned lessons of civilized society.

The level of fair process that we offer to individuals reflects our sense of decency and the depth of our conscience. On campus, as elsewhere, you have a moral right—and often a legal right—to decency and fundamental fairness. This *Guide to Due Process and Campus Justice* is about those rights. Behind the maze of legal language is a set of moral principles about how human beings may and may not treat one another.

DEFINITION: DUE PROCESS

An established course for judicial proceedings or other governmental activities designed to safeguard the legal rights of the individual.

—AMERICAN HERITAGE DICTIONARY

Part I: Introduction

If you face serious disciplinary action at a college or university, you are not alone. Thousands of students are tried in campus hearings each year, facing penalties that extend to suspension or expulsion. The bad news is that campus hearings often lack the kinds of basic fact-finding mechanisms and procedural safeguards that a decent society should provide. As a result, you run a significant risk of being found responsible for a minor or, indeed, serious offense—even if you are innocent. Offenses that are considered relatively minor in the criminal justice system are sometimes categorized as major on campus and can lead to severe punishment. The good news is that there is much that you can do to secure more fairness and to protect yourself and your future. Students facing disciplinary action at both public and private universities have certain rights. This *Guide* is designed to help you understand and exercise these rights.

Campus administrators—frequently advised by the institution's general counsel (*i.e.*, an attorney who works specifically for the institution)—often have far more information than students about the legal requirements of campus judicial systems and procedures. This *Guide* aims to change that. FIRE believes that students facing disciplinary tribunals should develop specific skills in preparing a defense. We believe that if you know your rights—and let your institution know that you will exercise them—you may be accorded a greater degree of procedural fairness.

How to Use This Guide

This *Guide* aims to help students accused of wrongdoing understand the procedural safeguards to which they are entitled. It also aims to provide tactical advice on how to secure these protections.

Part I explains what due process is and why it is so important to a free and decent society. Part II discusses due process at public universities generally; Part III discusses fair procedures at private universities. Part IV provides more detail about the specific procedural protections to which public university students are entitled. Part V discusses the changing protections afforded to students accused of sexual harassment and sexual assault.

Be advised: Every disciplinary proceeding has its own individual nuances and challenges. This *Guide* cannot anticipate them all. Every case is different, so making specific recommendations about strategy is difficult. Consequently, this *Guide* does not address, except broadly, the subject of how to prepare an effective defense. Instead, our focus is on how you can safeguard your right to be judged fairly.

(Please note: While this *Guide* discusses the law, your rights, and legal precedent in detail, it is not intended to provide formal legal advice. If you seek legal advice, we urge you to contact an attorney.)

Even if you have only a specific question, try to read the *Guide* in its entirety. You may have rights that you are not aware of—and using *all* of your rights is the best way to ensure a fair outcome in your case. Learn the relevant terms, and use them. It makes a difference when administrators know that you understand your rights and can state them in legal—or at least accurate—language. They suddenly wonder to whom you have been talking.

Your Rights If You Face Disciplinary Action

If you are a student at a *public* college or university and you face the possibility of serious punishment—expulsion, suspension, or some lesser but still significant sanction—you are entitled to certain protections under the Constitution's guarantee of "due process."

Because public colleges and universities are governmental institutions, their disciplinary proceedings are legally constrained in certain ways. Specifically, the Fifth and Fourteenth Amendments to the Constitution promise that the government will not deprive any person of "life, liberty, or property, without due process of law." This means that campus disciplinary proceedings must be handled in a standardized, consistent manner—that is, not in an arbitrary manner chosen for this or that particular case—and must include procedural safeguards that match the seriousness of the potential punishment.

The specific procedural protections to which due process entitles you depends on your particular situation. **In general, the more serious the charge and potential penalty, the greater the protections that must be given to you.** That's why traffic court offers fewer protections than a court that hears charges of serious crimes. This sliding scale also explains why students in campus disciplinary hearings don't receive all the rights granted to defendants in criminal trials: Imprisonment, for pretty good reason, is considered more serious than getting kicked out of school.

In any case involving suspension or expulsion for *disciplinary reasons*—as opposed to academic reasons—at a public university, you are entitled to *at least* the following protections:

- The right to have your case heard under regular (non-arbitrary) procedures used for all similar cases
- The right to receive notice of the charges against you
- The right to hear a description of the university's evidence against you
- The right to present your side of the story to an impartial arbiter or panel

You are entitled to the rights listed above in all cases involving disciplinary suspension or expulsion. As discussed in more detail in Part IV, you may also be entitled to other rights in certain cases, such as the right to have a lawyer present during your hearing or the right to review written records related to the charges beforehand.

These same rules do not apply, however, to public university students who face suspension or expulsion because of poor *academic* performance. Very few procedural safeguards are required in academic dismissals, because courts do not feel comfortable second-guessing academic judgments. All that due process requires in academic cases is that universities treat students in a manner that is careful and not arbitrary, that students be given a reasonable opportunity to present their defense or explanation, and that the school's own established rules and definitions be followed.

Unlike public universities, *private* universities are not part of the government and are not legally required to provide students constitutional due process. However, private universities are often contractually bound to follow their own established disciplinary processes. If a private university says that it will offer a certain safeguard, it is obligated to do so, more or less in the manner that any private party entering into a contract with another party would be obligated to fulfill that agreement. Breach of contract is both a moral and a legal wrong.

Public universities also are bound by contract law to follow their own rules. In other words, if a public university promises greater procedural protections than due process requires, it must actually give them to you. This is an important argument to remember when navigating your college's disciplinary system. We spend much of this *Guide* describing the *minimal* procedural protections guaranteed by the right to due process. But in many cases, the central issue is the university's promise to go *beyond* these rights. Promises matter, and students have considerable power in holding universities to their promises.

Finally, *both* public and private universities are bound

by a federal law that guarantees the privacy of student records, including disciplinary records. This law governs whether universities may disclose certain disciplinary convictions to certain parties—the police, for example, or the victim of the misconduct. Though this particular privacy law is not a part of due process, we briefly discuss it because it provides important protections to students accused of misconduct.

How to Prepare for Your Disciplinary Case

Your success in answering disciplinary charges depends on your preparation beforehand.

The most important step you can take is to thoroughly familiarize yourself with your institution's procedures as soon as possible. If you have done (or are suspected of having done) something that you believe might lead to a disciplinary proceeding, you should read your campus's disciplinary rules and procedures even before you are charged. In fact, it is good practice for *all* students to proactively familiarize themselves with their institutions' policies and procedures. Disciplinary charges often come as a surprise, and it is advantageous to know what to expect in advance.

You can usually find these rules in your university's student conduct code or student handbook. You need to know certain things before the process begins:

- How will you be notified if you are charged?
- How long will you have to prepare your defense?

- What opportunity will you have to present your case?
- Does your university offer more rights and protections than the minimal requirements set by due process?

Once you understand the university's rules, you can begin to plan your defense. Interview witnesses and collect evidence that may help you fight the charges. It is important to begin preparing your defense as early as possible—and certainly as soon as you receive notice that you have been charged. Speed is especially important if your university offers only a brief time before the hearing. Evidence and memories are at their freshest soon after an event.

How to Conduct an Investigation for Your Defense

The best way to get the bottom of any complex factual matter is a thorough investigation.

If you are involved in an incident that you think might lead to a complaint against you, immediately gather and preserve relevant evidence. It is best to be prepared just in case you are charged—especially because charges are often brought long after the incident, when memories have faded, witnesses have disappeared, and the trail of evidence is cold. You will want to be careful, however, that your manner of gathering evidence observes campus rules and does not provoke a formal accusation against you. If you think that the possibility of a formal accusation is particularly remote, it might be better to let things be.

If a complaint is threatened or brought, you should continue your investigation, or, if you have not yet started, you should begin work immediately. If your investigation requires interviewing witnesses, it may be best to have a lawyer, a trusted professor, or a professional investigator act on your behalf. That way, you may avoid allegations of "witness tampering." It is also useful to have your own witness present during an interview, in case the person interviewed later denies that he or she said something. When the interviewee is willing, you will want to record statements or have them written down.

You need to be active and to anticipate the benefits of conducting an investigation on your own behalf. Your goal is to persuade the university, by the weight and quality of your evidence, into dropping unfair charges against you or, if it comes to a hearing, into finding you innocent of false charges. The university is your adversary in a disciplinary case against you—however much you might want to think of it as your friend—and there is no guarantee that it will continue to look for evidence that may help you once it has found some evidence against you. Sometimes, it is in an administrator's interest to find a scapegoat for ills at the college or university. If you are charged with conduct that offends dominant sensibilities or ideologies on campus, there may be a tendency for the university to overlook evidence in your favor for political reasons. Providing the tribunal with a formal submission of evidence in your favor may refocus your case upon the actual facts.

If your investigation discovers facts overlooked by the administration's investigators that you wish to bring to the tribunal's attention, you should submit a statement detailing what the school would have learned had it conducted a more thorough investigation. This is somewhat analogous to what is known as an "offer of proof" in a legal proceeding, which is a statement of what the court would have determined if it had ruled differently on the exclusion of a piece of evidence.

University rules may not encourage formal submissions of this sort, or may even attempt to ban them outright. But if you make such a submission, the university will almost certainly read it. It does not want to be indifferent to facts and to the possibility of innocence. Even if the university disciplinary committee *does* refuse to read your submission, you have established a record of both your good faith and the committee's bad faith. Further, you can force the university to include your submission of evidence in the file of your disciplinary case. As discussed in Part IV, universities must accept and include in a student's file student submissions correcting alleged factual inaccuracies in the file. It is a particularly good idea to provide this sort of submission if you are unable to participate in your disciplinary hearing.

Regardless of the structure of your university's disciplinary process, you should never let an inadequate investigation by the administration hurt your case. If there is something you found that the administration hasn't uncovered, confront them with it. Let them know that your evidence is there—and that, if necessary, it will be public knowledge at some point.

CRIME, EDUCATION, AND PUNISHMENT

To excuse the fact that students are often afforded minimal due process protections at best, college and university administrators often argue that campus discipline is "educational" rather than punitive. They insist that instituting "formal" procedures or "legalistic" protections is inappropriate because of the "pedagogical" character of the disciplinary process.

But this argument ignores the fact that, in serious cases, campus justice is truly punitive. Expulsion from a university is life-altering. Suspensions and other punishments that disrupt a student's education are serious penalties that impact a student's educational, professional, and social prospects for years. Worse still, such harsh sanctions are often imposed for offenses that would be minor in the criminal justice system.

All punishment is necessarily "educational" in some sense; people learn a lesson from being punished, for good or for ill. It is the type of "lesson" learned that counts, however. The student who has learned that he or she is powerless to protect him- or herself from arbitrary discipline has fared far worse than the student who has learned the value of due process protections by being tried in a fair, consistent hearing process.

Just because a student being punished is also "learning" doesn't lessen the need for fair procedures to ensure that only the guilty are disciplined. Procedural protections exist because history has proven that without them, people who have power will abuse the rights of the powerless and that many innocent people will be hurt in the process. If students learn that important lesson via the disciplinary process, then society has been well served.

Retaining an Attorney

Many students ask if they should retain a lawyer to help fight disciplinary charges. The answer, predictably, depends on the circumstances.

If you think that you may face criminal charges for the same conduct that led to your campus disciplinary charge, it is *absolutely crucial* to have an attorney. Anything that you say to the university's disciplinary committee can be used against you in criminal court, so you should consult a lawyer before making any statements whatsoever.

On the other hand, if it is unlikely that you will also face criminal charges, it is really up to you to decide whether retaining legal counsel is worthwhile. Having a competent lawyer certainly can't hurt you. But other people at your college, such as informed and sympathetic professors or residence advisors, may actually have *more* experience with the disciplinary process than nonuniversity attorneys, and they will almost always work free of charge. Indeed, at some campuses, students have formed groups specifically to assist their peers throughout the disciplinary process. For example, at Ohio University, the student organization Students Defending Students provides free assistance to those facing campus charges, advising them with regard to their rights, past punishments for similar offenses, and how best to navigate the stress of being accused of misconduct.

Further, university advisors may be more warmly received by administrators conducting the hearing process who might otherwise feel threatened or defensive around an attorney. Be careful, however. Campus advisors, especially administrators, may well have a conflict of interest. Their primary loyalty—personally and, often, legally—may be to the university rather than to you. If you are facing charges that could result in significant disruption to, or termination of, your academic career, you should carefully consider hiring an attorney to assist you. The more serious the offense, the more thought should be given to retaining counsel.

Some colleges and universities have arranged with local attorneys to provide limited legal services (sometimes free of charge) to students facing both campus and criminal charges. Check to see if your institution or your student government provides such a service. If so, discussing your case with the attorneys on staff may be a cost-effective and simple way to begin to prepare your defense, particularly if they have experience with the types of charges you are facing. Be sure to ask about the limitations of their assistance, however, as not all student legal service offices can handle every case or are able to provide formal legal representation and the attorney-client privilege of confidentiality.

How to Fight for Fair Treatment

Throughout this *Guide*, we will discuss students who have sued their colleges after being denied due process. Talking about past cases is useful because the requirements for due process on campus have emerged from the accumulated decisions of the courts. These past decisions are known as *precedents*. Talking about precedents is the best way to describe the current state of student due process rights.

This *Guide*'s discussion of legal precedent should not be taken as a suggestion that filing a lawsuit is always a good idea. In fact, only a handful of student disciplinary cases ever reach the point where it would be reasonable to file suit. And even in cases where lawsuits are possible, they are often a bad idea. Lawsuits can last many years and may cost you tens of thousands of dollars—and often, the best possible outcome is simply a new campus hearing. That new hearing might allow you to present evidence and to make your arguments under fairer circumstances, but it will not necessarily achieve your vindication. On the other hand, if the university's mistreatment of you has been objectively outrageous, if the evidence of your innocence is strong but was ignored, and if the precedents in your judicial district are favorable to students' rights, a lawsuit might indeed be a realistic alternative.

Lawsuits aren't always necessary to secure due process protections and a fair hearing. Sometimes, you can receive the procedural protections you need just by asking for them. If you believe that your university's disciplinary procedures are preventing you from mounting an effective defense, explain the problem—politely but firmly—to the responsible administrators. For example, if the university gives you only ten days' notice of the

COURT DECISIONS ABOUT SCHOOL DISCIPLINE DIFFER BY PLACE

This *Guide* refers to cases decided by many different courts. Technically, the rulings of a court are binding only on future cases in the same court (or in a lower court in the same appellate jurisdiction). Opinions of the Supreme Court of the United States are the only cases binding throughout the entire country. It would be ideal, of course, if you (or your lawyer) found that your college was in a jurisdiction with a useful precedent. Most of the time, however, you will need to rely on the persuasive value of the decisions we describe, not on their binding authority.

date of your disciplinary hearing, and you have a busy schedule, an illness, or pressing personal or family obligations during that period, your first course of action should be to talk to the administrators and explain the problem. It is usually best, at first, to appeal to reason, common sense, and basic notions of fairness rather than to legal rules. In many cases, the administration will accommodate your request.

Make sure any requests you make of administrators are either in writing or confirmed in writing. In order to create a written record of an oral request, it is very important to follow up a discussion with a polite and informal letter or email, restating both what you asked for and the reasons for your request. In the event that an administrator has replied to your request orally, it is likewise crucial to follow up with an email to that administrator confirming your understanding of the discussion. Using email to correspond with those involved in the disciplinary process makes it easy to document your requests and discussions, without making it quite so obvious that you are keeping a written record.

There are two things that you can do if the university refuses to grant your request. First, submit a written letter to the appropriate administrator about what you would have shown if the safeguard you requested had been granted. For example, if the university tells you that you may not speak to a crucial witness during your investigation, you should submit a statement in writing about what this interview, if allowed to proceed, would have shown. For one thing, that statement will be part of the record, and the fact-finders may manage to see it anyway. For another, if later you *do* have to go to court, the judge will see what you could have proven had you been given a fair opportunity.

Second, if you think that you are being a denied a protection that is critical to your case, consider a threat, indirect or direct, of legal action. Many students find that it is most effective to suggest the possibility of legal action subtly, before any suit. Informally tell the administrators responsible for your case that you believe the university's disciplinary procedures to be unlawful and explain why, using language and precedent you've learned from this *Guide*. Administrators fear potentially embarrassing and costly lawsuits, and the mere hint of legal action may be enough to convince administrators to grant you the protections you require.

FIVE STEPS TO DEFENDING YOURSELF

When faced with a disciplinary charge:

1. Carefully review your student handbook, disciplinary code, and other campus policies that apply to you or to your organization.

2. Read this *Guide* in its entirety—and then re-read the sections most applicable to your case and to your type of university.

3. Take careful notes of conversations. Send emails that restate the conversations that you have had. Keep copies of any written correspondence with administrators, faculty members, or student leaders.

4. Obtain an advisor or lawyer who can help you navigate the disciplinary process.

5. Give your disciplinary hearing first priority and prepare for it well in advance.

If this informal approach fails, you can formally threaten legal action in writing. If you have a good basis for a lawsuit and threaten to bring one, the administration may well back down. Colleges often find it wiser to settle *before* a lawsuit is filed rather than face legal fees, wasted time, negative publicity, the embarrassment of a public record of their unfairness, and the possibility of creating a bad legal precedent for themselves. The university may step back when you let it know that it is violating the law, making it unnecessary for you to take the final step of securing legal counsel and filing suit.

But if requests and demands for due process and threats to sue fail, and if you have the facts and the law on your side, you should indeed sue your university. Be advised, however: Campus due process lawsuits can be very difficult, extremely expensive, and longer than you'd expect. While some types of rights-based college litigation are relatively straightforward and speedy—facial challenges to unconstitutional college speech codes, for example—due process suits are not. When faced with a campus due process suit, college administrators might compromise or settle with you fairly early. However, they might not. Universities usually get "free" legal representation from the state, their general counsel, or outside attorneys—that is, paid by either taxpayers or student tuitions—so they have a financial advantage over you if the case takes years to resolve, as many do. If your case presents an important issue or involves an egregious denial of due process protections, however, you may be able to obtain skilled representation from a variety of civil liberties organizations and legal foundations. Be sure to submit your case to FIRE via our website at www.thefire.org. We can't help in every instance, but if your case would benefit from an attorney, we may be able to refer it to our Legal Network, a national collection of attorneys dedicated to protecting student and faculty rights on campus.

PART II: DUE PROCESS AT PUBLIC UNIVERSITIES

Due Process in American Law

To receive the fundamentally fair procedures to which you are entitled, you need a basic understanding of (1) due process in the non-university criminal justice system and (2) the legal and moral theories behind the ways due process does and does not apply to college disciplinary procedures.

Due process has evolved over the centuries as a way to ensure that accusatory proceedings produce accurate and truthful results. This is one of the most vital components of a free, decent, and fair society. The accumulated experience of countless cases—dating all the way back to medieval England—has taught us that due process (*i.e.*, the process that is "due" or "owed" to each citizen) is essential to ensure the best chance of learning the truth during the trial process.

For example, we have learned that juries stand the best chance of getting to the bottom of complicated factual matters if the accused or her lawyer is given an opportunity to ask questions of the accuser and of hostile witnesses. How comfortable does an accusing witness appear as he or she looks the accused in the eye and testifies? How credibly does the accusing witness respond to hard questions posed by a skilled cross-examiner? These are not "technicalities," but rather the essential components of fair decisions and justice. The jurisprudence of due process is concerned with identifying specific procedures that are actually effective in discovering the truth.

Procedural Due Process

Procedural due process is a legal term that refers to the specific rules that govern how an accusatory proceeding is carried out—in other words, the steps by which a case is "tried" in order to determine the truth or falsity of an accusation. For example, procedural due process includes the rules governing the accused's rights to question witnesses who testify against him, as well as a defendant's right to be tried by a jury of her peers. These protections reflect society's solemn commitment to the importance of obtaining an accurate result when a citizen stands accused. (While *procedural* due process rights are of greatest interest to you as a student accused of a disciplinary infraction, due process also confers another set of rights—*substantive* due process rights—which are defined and discussed later in Part II.)

The right to procedural due process in contemporary America comes from the Fifth and Fourteenth Amendments to the United States Constitution. The Fifth Amendment's due process clause limits the power of the *federal* government and its institutions, while the Fourteenth Amendment's due process clause restricts the power of *state* governments. As a practical matter, most of the restrictions on the federal government's power over the rights of citizens also apply through the Fourteenth Amendment to state government.

A common misconception is that due process protections apply only in the context of criminal trials. In fact, these constitutional provisions guarantee that the federal and state governments, respectively, may not deprive any person "of life, liberty, or property, without due process of law." In the educational context, your interest in your diploma and in the value of a clear academic record establishes a property right, and your interest in your reputation and good name establishes a liberty right.

Each of the tens of thousands of court opinions that have interpreted these constitutional guarantees basically proceeds in a simple two-step manner:

First, the court looks to see whether due process applies—that is, whether a person's life, liberty, or property is at risk because of something the government is doing.

Second, if the person is entitled to due process, the court determines what process is due to the defendant under the particular circumstances.

Due process is flexible. How much process is due to the accused depends largely on the context. As the Supreme Court held in *Mathews v. Eldridge* (1976), courts must consider three factors to see what particular protections are required in a given situation:

1. What's at stake for the accused? What does she or he stand to lose if found guilty?
2. Under the current procedures, how significant is the risk that the accused will be wrongly punished? Would more safeguards reduce this risk?
3. How costly and time-consuming would the new protections be for the government?

Some situations, such as the criminal trial of a person charged with murder, obviously require the greatest due process. A guilty finding may result in the defendant's being deprived of liberty or even life. Since the stakes are so high, society has a clear interest in making sure a just, reliable result is reached. Other situations, like contesting tickets in traffic court, require far, far fewer procedural protections. Disciplinary tribunals for public college students fall somewhere between these two poles. While still significant, the stakes in college hearings are lower than those in criminal hearings, and it would be costly and time-consuming for colleges to afford students all the rights afforded criminal defendants. Still other situations, such a student facing suspension for poor academic performance, require even fewer safeguards, as courts have generally taken a hands-off approach to colleges' academic decision-making.

Procedural Protections in Disciplinary Cases

University officials often say that college disciplinary proceedings are "educational," not punitive. As a result, they argue that students in college disciplinary proceedings are not entitled to procedural protections. But courts have disagreed. The law is clear: Due process protections are required for students facing disciplinary hearings at public universities. As noted above, people are entitled to due process rights whenever they have "liberty" or "property" interests at stake—and both interests are most certainly at stake in public university disciplinary hearings.

Liberty and Property Interests

The Supreme Court of the United States has held that "liberty interests" are involved (lawyers would say "implicated") whenever a person's good name, reputation, honor, or integrity is at stake. When a disciplinary board finds a student guilty of non-academic misconduct, the impact can be devastating for his or her future—academically, professionally, and even socially. An expulsion from college isn't as serious as a prison sentence in terms of deprivation of liberty, but there's no question that it can have a profound impact on the rest of a student's life.

College disciplinary hearings implicate a student's "property interests" as well. The progress that a student has made toward a degree constitutes property—a thing of value that belongs to a person—because of all the time and money that he or she has invested in progressing towards that degree. Once the state has chosen to grant students a property right by admitting them to a public institution of higher education, it cannot revoke this right arbitrarily or unfairly.

Students facing disciplinary hearings at public colleges and universities, thus, have *both* liberty and property interests at stake.

The more serious the possible deprivations of liberty and property—generally, the more serious the accusation—the greater the due process protections required. Most of our discussion focuses on the protections due to students facing possible suspension or expulsion, but liberty and property are also at stake in cases involving more minor potential punishments. Students are entitled to a different kind of due process, with fewer procedural protections, in cases involving only minor sanctions. There are some cases where the potential deprivations of liberty and property are so minor that very little or no process is due. The courts have not laid out precisely where this threshold lies in the university context, and the law continues to evolve on this question.

Substantive Due Process Rights

In addition to *procedural* due process rights, you also possess a separate class of rights known as *substantive* due process rights. Substantive due process rights protect you from vague, overbroad, and unfair rules. In the American understanding of justice, no person may have any of his or her fundamental rights or personal freedoms taken away without both procedural *and* substantive due process. Public colleges and universities may not improperly restrict these substantive due process rights by establishing vague or unfair rules that can be sprung upon you unfairly or that can be interpreted, unfairly and surprisingly, to cover seemingly ordinary conduct.

DEFINITION: SUBSTANTIVE DUE PROCESS RIGHTS

Substantive due process rights are those that protect a party from unreasonable, excessive, or uncivilized treatment or punishment. Freedom from punishment for certain personal decisions and freedom from invasion of privacy are examples of such rights.

Disciplinary Cases Involving Suspension or Expulsion

Students facing possible suspension or expulsion from public colleges and universities are entitled to due process protections because their liberty and property are at stake. But exactly what process is due?

At the absolute minimum, students in campus disciplinary cases are entitled to have (1) notice of the charges against them, (2) an explanation of the evidence against them, and (3) an opportunity to tell their side of the story.

The Supreme Court established these minimal requirements in *Goss v. Lopez* (1975), in which nine suspended

Ohio high school students sued their school, claiming that they had been denied due process. The Court, weighing the costs and benefits to the school and to the students, held that although the most severe suspensions were only ten days long, the students had constitutional rights protected by the due process clause of the Fourteenth Amendment.

The *Goss* Court ruled that in student disciplinary cases involving short suspensions, an accused student must "be given oral or written notice of the charges against him and, if he denies them, an explanation of the evidence the authorities have and an opportunity to present his side of the story." The Court held that, *at the very least*, administrators must engage in an "informal give-and-take" with a student before imposing a penalty. To the Court, requiring this bare minimum of due process—notice and an "informal hearing" that permits a student to "give his version of the events"—is necessary because it "will provide a meaningful hedge against erroneous action."

Isn't *Goss* a High School Case?

It is. As a college student, you should generally consult *college* cases to understand the full scope of your rights. But high school cases are very useful to you, too, because as a college student, you have *at least* the same rights that high school students possess. Courts have generally found that college students are entitled to *more* due process protections than students in the lower grades because college students are adults in the eyes of the law. Further, because there are more high school than college students, high school jurisprudence may be better developed on the point at issue in your case. In other words, high school legal precedents establish a *floor*, not a *ceiling*, to the rights accorded to you as a college student.

Importantly, the Court specifically stated that in more difficult cases, administrators may permit the participation or advice of counsel, hold hearings, or allow cross-examination. To a certain extent, *Goss* left the decision of whether to offer these greater protections to the "discretion" of administrators. But the Court also stated that due process "may require more formal procedures" in more serious cases.

Goss remains the Supreme Court's clearest statement on student due process rights. So in the four decades following *Goss*, the lower federal courts and various state courts have worked on a case-by-case basis to determine how much process is due in various situations. While results have varied, federal and state courts have agreed that the amount of due process required in campus disciplinary cases must be based on the nature and gravity of the charges, and on the range and severity of the potential punishments.

Exactly what protections are required in particular cases, however, remains unsettled. Courts have required protections such as cross-examination and the right to an attorney in some campus cases where they have judged these safeguards to be necessary for basic fairness. But courts have also denied them in other cases where they believed that students could get a fundamentally fair hearing without these protections.

Generally speaking, judges must weigh the costs and benefits, for the institution and for the parties involved, in each particular case. The cost of adding procedural safeguards—in terms of time, effort, money, and inter-ference with the smooth operation of the university—must be balanced against the likelihood of grave error or injustice if the procedural safeguards were not offered.

Under this analysis, you should insist on stricter pro-cedural protections in cases involving or even touching upon freedom of speech. Constitutionally protected vital rights are the foundation of our liberty, and when they are at stake, the need for fair procedure is at its most critical.

Several factors have kept the courts from establishing more specific rules. First, due process by its very nature is supposed to be flexible. The establishment of one-size-fits-all rules would be contrary to the constitutional premise that one has a right only to the process that is "due." (It's worth pointing out that the classic legal trea-tise on due process by Judge Henry Friendly is titled *Some Kind of Hearing.*)

Second, only a relatively small number of campus due process cases have reached the courts. It will take more cases to smooth out the differences in how various ju-risdictions treat the same situation. The law is likely to remain in flux with regard to exactly what protections public college students may expect in their disciplin-ary hearings. This is particularly true because of the increased regulatory and legislative activity related to campus discipline in recent years. As federal agencies and federal and state lawmakers pass new rules and regulations governing how colleges must respond to certain misconduct—particularly sexual assault—courts will continue to clarify what the Fifth and Fourteenth Amendments mean for students in campus disciplinary hearings at public institutions.

Third, courts are generally very reluctant to interfere with the internal affairs of a college. For decades, judges have recognized the importance of "academic freedom"— which can be loosely defined as the right of colleges to make academic decisions for themselves, free from government interference. No interpretation of academic freedom, however, gives higher education the right to break the law or violate students' constitutional rights.

The law is unsettled, and even a bit conflicted. But it's still possible to get a general sense of how courts approach campus due process. Part IV of this *Guide* reviews the state of the law with respect to particular procedural safeguards.

Procedural Protections in Academic Cases

So far we have spoken only about disciplinary cases. Students who face suspension or expulsion because of poor academic performance are also entitled to due process, but only minimal protections are required. Universities must make academic decisions in a manner that is careful and not arbitrary, but they do not have to grant students the same procedural safeguards required in disciplinary matters.

Academic cases require fewer procedural protections because professors, almost by definition, are better equipped than judges to make academic evaluations. The procedural protections of the criminal law are useful for fact-finding, but are not required in cases involving subjective judgments of academic performance. A professor's grading of a student's academic performance is protected from court interference by the principle of academic freedom. Unless the professor's assessment can be shown to have been influenced by improper factors, such as the student's race or political viewpoint, the professor's decision is final.

The Supreme Court considered the balance between academic freedom and due process in two major cases of the late 1970s and early 1980s. In *Board of Curators of the University of Missouri v. Horowitz* (1978), the Court reviewed a due process claim brought by a student who was dismissed from a public medical school because of poor academic performance. The student was never given an opportunity to be heard by any of the university committees that took up her case. However, the Court held that hearings and associated procedural protections are not required in academic dismissal cases, because they do not involve the kind of factual determinations in which heightened protections would be useful. The Court ruled that Horowitz's treatment was consistent with due process because of a few basic conditions: her work had been thoroughly reviewed by both faculty members and school committees, and the decision to dismiss her was "careful and deliberate"; she had been given ample notice that her work was judged to be unsatisfactory; and she had been granted a number of chances to exhibit improvement.

The Supreme Court expanded on this in *Regents of the University of Michigan v. Ewing* (1985), in which a student claimed that he was denied due process when he was dismissed from a medical program after receiving the lowest score ever recorded on a standardized test in the history of that program. He complained that many other students with even poorer overall academic records had been allowed to retake the standardized test. In refusing to interfere with the expulsion, the Court invoked the principle of academic freedom. It ruled that courts should defer to universities' judgments on *academic matters* unless there is "such a substantial departure from accepted academic norms as to demonstrate that the person or committee responsible did not actually exercise professional judgment." Because the student's overall record was exceptionally poor, the university's decision to dismiss him was well within its discretion.

Lower courts have interpreted these decisions to require that public colleges and universities make academic decisions in a manner that is "careful and deliberate," or at least not "arbitrary and capricious." In other words, if a public college can show that it is expelling you because of your academic performance, and not some other reason, chances are that a judge will side with the college.

Courts will intervene in academic decisions only if you were treated with blatant unfairness or were punished on the basis of prohibited factors and criteria. If you made a clear case that the academic sanctions against you had no basis in reason or fact—or arose from other grudges held against you—you then might convince a court to set aside its presumption in favor of the university. For example, in *Alcorn v. Vaksman* (1994), the Court of Appeals of Texas ordered a public university to readmit an expelled graduate student. The court ruled that the dismissal was made on the basis of personal hostility arising from the student's intellectual disagreements with the faculty and his outspoken criticism of university policies—not on the basis of the student's erratic (but occasionally distinguished) academic record.

Additionally, courts have sometimes required that students be given advance notice that their poor performance has placed their status in jeopardy, or, failing that, be given notice of the general standard of performance expected of students.

Cheating: The Border Between Academic and Disciplinary Offenses

Cheating—the use of fraud or deception to enhance one's academic performance—stands at the boundary of the academic and disciplinary realms.

Sometimes, for due process purposes, cases of cheating are best considered as disciplinary cases. For instance, when a student is accused of copying from another student's paper by looking over his shoulder during an exam, determining guilt or innocence is a matter of fact-finding: Did the student actually copy? If the facts indicate that a rule was broken, the student is guilty; if they do not, the student is innocent. The procedural protections of due process are designed to assist with precisely these sorts of factual determinations and to help the university find out what happened as fairly as possible.

In contrast, charges of plagiarism—a form of cheating—include both academic and disciplinary elements. On the one hand, the real question in a plagiarism case is whether a student committed the particular act of using someone else's work without attribution. That is a factual question. On the other hand, the question of whether a student's words were so close to those of another, un-cited source that his or her work constitutes plagiarism also requires skilled academic judgment. The issue to be resolved in a campus plagiarism case is thus both factual *and* judgmental.

When you seek a court's intervention, it is in your interest to define the charge as "disciplinary," offering you more safeguards. It is in the interest of the school's administrators and lawyers to define the charge as "academic," offering them greater discretionary power. Sometimes that line is quite vague, as in the case of plagiarism. Having your case treated as disciplinary in the campus proceedings themselves would create a record that strengthens your argument in court that the case is indeed a disciplinary rather than an academic matter.

The University Must Deliver What It Promises

A public college or university cannot decide on its own not to grant the due process rights that the Constitution requires. The Constitution *mandates* these rights. If your college or university denies you *any* of the required due process protections, you can file a due process claim in federal or state court.

Many public colleges and universities, however, promise students considerably *more* than due process requires. The law does not oblige campuses to offer a full and formal judicial hearing, for example, but some universities provide something fairly close to one. Courts do not typically require campus tribunals to permit cross-examination of witnesses, with some exceptions based on the type of case at issue, but some universities have chosen to allow it in certain circumstances.

Courts will generally compel both public and private universities to give you all of the procedural protections that they have promised you. The courts enforce these obligations, however, not as a matter of your rights to due process, but as a right you have under state contract law. Some states also have rules that require administrative agencies to follow their own regulations. If you live in such a state, these administrative rules may provide an additional legal theory useful to force a public university to obey its own rules.

The case of *Morrison v. University of Oregon Health Sciences Center* (1984), decided by the Court of Appeals of Oregon, illustrates the potential advantages of making a

38

contract or state administrative procedure claim, rather than a due process claim, if your university deviates from the rules it established for itself. The issue in *Morrison* was whether a university had followed its own procedures when it dismissed a dental student for academic reasons. The university's policy stated that only evidence raised at a student's actual hearing could be considered in reaching such a decision, but the record showed that the university had considered evidence never raised at this hearing. The court ordered the university to reverse a dismissal that had been reached by a violation of its own promised procedures. This victory could not have been gained on due process grounds, because due process does not *require* universities to grant students a hearing in academic cases.

If your public college or university denies you basic procedural protections guaranteed by the Constitution, you may have a due process claim. If your college or university—public or private—fails to follow its own rules, you may have a claim under several other legal doctrines, including state precedent about contracts that oblige organizations to honor their own promises.

PART III: PROCEDURAL FAIRNESS AT PRIVATE UNIVERSITIES

Public universities, as an arm of the government, are constrained by the Constitution in setting rules and disciplining students. Private colleges and universities are free, by contrast, to set their own rules and to formulate their own disciplinary procedures within very wide guidelines and boundaries established by state laws. A student is free to take or not to take such procedures into account when deciding to attend such an institution. Once private institutions publish disciplinary rules, however, they are then obligated by principles of contract law to follow them in good faith, even if not always to the strict letter.

Private Universities Generally Must Follow Their Established Procedures

Private universities are not legally required to promise fair procedures to their students. However, nearly all universities have student handbooks and manuals that set out rules and standards for their student judicial systems. Courts in many states have held that these rules and standards form a contract of sorts, and that universities must live up to them in at least a general way.

The legal requirement that universities actually give students the rights they promise stems from a variety of doctrines, above all from the law of contracts. The basic principle of contract law is also one that lies at the heart of morality: People have to live up to their reciprocal promises. If one party agrees to a contract and doesn't honor it, a court can force that party to do so and can award monetary damages to the other party. If you agree to attend a university and pay tuition and fees, and you do so relying upon the rules and regulations that the university tells you it has established, then a deal of sorts has been struck, roughly like a legal contract. In the same way you must pay your tuition, the university must deliver the due process protections it promises you in its policies.

Courts have often held that the representations universities make in their student handbooks about the disciplinary process are promises that they must keep. However, courts do not enforce these promises as strictly as other kinds of contracts. For example, courts typically have not awarded students monetary damages when colleges simply fail to follow their disciplinary rules. In addition, they tend to give universities leeway if they have followed their rules in a general way, even if not to the letter. The consensus of the courts is that the relationship between a student and a university has, as one judge put it, a "strong, albeit flexible, contractual flavor," and that the promises made in handbooks have to be "substantially observed."

Some states follow an ancient "common law" doctrine—not embodied in any statute, but followed by courts on the basis of longstanding practice and precedent—that binds private organizations to treat their members with at least a minimal level of fairness and decency. This doctrine reinforces the contract law rules requiring universities to follow their own procedures.

Even though courts have not held that universities must adhere exactly to their rules, you can sometimes use the mere threat of a lawsuit to force your university to follow its own rules more closely. Colleges and universities fear lawsuits, especially when they are coupled with the prospect of bad publicity or when they are very likely in the wrong. If you make it clear that you know your rights, your university is less likely to place itself in a gray area of possible breach of contract by straying too far from its promises.

You also can use the fact that your university itself set the terms of its student handbook to your advantage. When a contract, or a contract-like agreement, is formulated by what the law terms the "stronger party," and the "weaker party" does not have an opportunity to negotiate specific terms, courts will lean in favor of the weaker party (here, the student) in resolving any ambiguities in the contract. Under this standard—applied to higher education, for example, in the U.S. District Court for the District of Columbia case of *Giles v. Howard University* (1977)—courts will interpret rules in a student handbook with whatever meaning the university should reasonably expect students to give them.

"DISCOVERY" AND CIVIL SUITS: UNIVERSITIES AND THE COURT OF PUBLIC OPINION

One reason why universities fear lawsuits involves what the law terms "discovery," which occurs before the start of a civil trial. During discovery, the university must produce for you and your lawyer all of the information relevant to your case. This can include email, administrative correspondence, internal documents, question-and-answer sessions conducted under oath with potential witnesses ("depositions"), or other evidence. Once this information is submitted as evidence or as an exhibit to a filing, it generally becomes a public record. This information is not just essential to your legal case—it may also prove embarrassing to the university if it reveals unfairness or even malice. Universities sometimes treat their students in ways that they would be ashamed to reveal to the general public, even if their behavior broke no laws. Therefore, universities are sometimes frightened of defending claims when doing so would reveal that they acted in an unfair or outrageous manner.

Breach of Contract Lawsuits

If you sue your university for breach of contract in a jurisdiction with precedents favorable to student rights, the court will review the student handbook and the record of your trial to see if the university failed to meet your reasonable expectations and therefore violated its contract with you.

Courts have generally held that colleges don't have to fulfill every obligation established in their own policies in exactly the way a student wants. Rather, a college needs only to "substantially" satisfy the conditions set out in its student handbook. So it's difficult to win a suit if the university can argue plausibly that it honored its promises in some general way. For example, in the Massachusetts Supreme Judicial Court case of *Schaer v. Brandeis* (2000), a student sued Brandeis University for, among other things, failing to produce a summary report of his disciplinary hearing, as promised by the student handbook. Brandeis had summarized the five-hour hearing in a mere twelve lines of text. The Massachusetts Supreme Judicial Court ruled that although it would be *better* to have issued a more complete summary, Brandeis's published procedures never had stated *precisely* how detailed a summary it would produce. Therefore, the court held, the twelve-line summary did not break the university's promise to the student. As you might conclude, courts do not always reach decisions that most ordinary citizens would find fair. (Even in *Schaer*, the university lost in the intermediate appellate court and won by only a single vote in the Supreme Judicial Court.)

However, when your university has obviously failed to live up to its obligations to you, then you have a real chance of winning in court. For example, in the case of *Fellheimer v. Middlebury College* (1994), the U.S. District Court for the District of Vermont cleared the disciplinary record of a Middlebury College student who had been found innocent of rape by the campus court but who was instead found guilty of "disrespect for persons." The student had never even been notified that he was being charged with that offense. But Middlebury's handbook not only promised that accused students would be informed of the charges against them, it also promised they would receive notice "with sufficient particularity to permit [them] to prepare to meet the charges." Middlebury told Fellheimer that he was charged with rape, but he was not told that he was also being charged with "disrespect for persons." He learned about that second charge only when the university found him guilty of it. The district court noted that Middlebury, a private college not bound by due process requirements, was under no constitutional obligation to tell its students of the charges against them. But as the court observed, Middlebury had nonetheless agreed to do so and to provide a fundamentally fair hearing. By failing to provide notice, it had failed to fulfill its promises in Fellheimer's case.

"This Is Not a Contract": University Disclaimers May Be Invalid

Sadly, as the law has increasingly required our institutions of higher education to live up to their promises, universities have sought new ways to avoid following the rules that they advertise. Many universities, acting on the advice of their lawyers, now add disclaimers to their student manuals, stating that they are not required to adhere to them or reserving the right to change them at any time. Some college and university handbooks now state specifically that the procedures they set forth should not be viewed by students as contractual promises. In the Fellheimer case, for example, Middlebury's handbook stated that the procedures were only to be adhered to "as faithfully as possible." Such language may give universities additional leeway, but—as seen in the Middlebury case—it does *not* allow universities to ignore their own rules. Your university is less likely to stray from its promises to you if it knows that you are aware of your right to judicial relief if it does so.

You should also know that the preamble to your university's disciplinary code may help you establish that your university's failure to meet its promises violates its own rules, even when your university promises merely to follow its procedures "as faithfully as possible." Why? Many preambles explicitly guarantee "fundamental fairness" or "integrity and impartiality" in campus hearings. So even if your university's handbook contains an escape clause ("as faithfully as possible"), you can make a strong case that the university was so unfaithful to its own published rules that it broke its overarching promise to offer fair procedures.

Statements in student handbooks that a college's rules do not constitute a contract are sometimes legally irrelevant—but not always, depending on how your state's courts have ruled on the issue. In any event, you should argue against their application. Universities plainly intend their student handbooks to set forth rules governing university discipline. These promises cannot reasonably be interpreted as mere fluff, meant only to convince students to attend the particular college. After all, if you and your fellow students are required to adhere to the rules of conduct set forth in the handbook as if it were a contract, the university has some obligation to do the same. Many judges would not take kindly to a college's effort to escape its obligations by claiming that its apparent promise is not really binding.

Private Universities May Not Be "Arbitrary and Capricious"

Many courts agree with the general proposition that disciplinary procedures at private colleges and universities may not be "arbitrary and capricious." This protection flows from old common law ideas about how private associations must treat their members. Over the years, our society has learned the value of protecting individuals from the arbitrary acts of other individuals, even in private associations. Courts differ, however, on just how unfair a university's disciplinary process must be before it is unlawful under this principle. Some courts prohibit disciplinary conclusions reached "without any discernable rational basis," and some bar those "made without substantial evidence" or "contrary to substantial evidence." The important thing to remember is that even when a private college does not promise fair practices in its student handbook, other legal doctrines beyond contract law are available to place some limit on just how unfairly a college may treat a student.

The doctrine prohibiting "arbitrary and capricious" discipline also prevents universities from disciplining students maliciously or dishonestly. A protection from arbitrary punishment is also a protection from discipline meted out with an outrageous or improper purpose.

That's the good news. The sobering news is that no matter how courts in your jurisdiction define "arbitrary and capricious," winning a case based on such a claim turns out to be very difficult in practice. While courts may conduct detailed reviews of a student's claim that a university's disciplinary procedures are arbitrary and capricious, such claims are generally unsuccessful. Courts tend to harbor broad respect for the self-government of private associations, including private colleges and universities. Nevertheless, the arbitrary and capricious rule is an important safeguard, because it prevents administrators from establishing truly outrageous disciplinary rules. Without it, there would be nothing to prohibit a private institution from flipping a coin to determine a student's guilt or innocence. Besides, the mere presence of a legal doctrine placing some limit on an institution's power, even where that limit is not clearly drawn, often has the effect of restraining the arrogance of power.

Courts will intervene when discipline at private universities is without any basis in reason whatsoever. For example, in the case of *Babcock v. New Orleans Baptist Theological Seminary* (1989), the Court of Appeal of Louisiana determined that a religious seminary had decided not to grant a degree to a student in a manner that was "grossly unfair and arbitrary." As a result, the court ordered the university to award the student the degree.

The student had encountered previous disciplinary problems at the seminary, but had been allowed to complete his coursework and had received notice of his impending graduation. Eleven days before graduation, however, the institution notified the student of its decision not to graduate him under a broad rule allowing it to withhold degrees from those "unfit" to receive them. The institution made this last-minute choice despite the fact that the student had already secured a court order prohibiting the seminary from punishing him further for his earlier difficulties. In reviewing the student's claim, the court held that because the institution gave no explanation for why the student was suddenly "unfit," and because the institution's graduation policy contained "due process infirmities" (for example, it failed to provide for notice and a hearing), the institution's discipline was "arbitrary and unjust" and could not stand.

DEFINITIONS: ARBITRARY AND CAPRICIOUS

Arbitrary: Determined by chance, whim, or impulse, and not by necessity, reason, or principle.

Capricious: Characterized by or subject to whim; impulsive and unpredictable.

—AMERICAN HERITAGE DICTIONARY

State Protections for Speech at Private Colleges

Too often, students and student groups face discipline not for conduct, but for "offensive" speech. Private universities are not bound by the First Amendment and therefore are generally not prohibited by law in most states from imposing discipline for mere speech. But there are important exceptions.

The United States Constitution does not prohibit private organizations, such as universities, from making rules limiting the speech of those who choose to join them. Some *state* constitutions, however, establish an "affirmative right" to free speech that belongs to every citizen. In states with such provisions, courts have sometimes ruled that there are limits to the blanket rules that private colleges may make restricting speech.

In *State of New Jersey v. Schmid* (1980), for example, the New Jersey Supreme Court ruled that a guarantee in the state constitution that "[e]very person may freely speak ... on all subjects" barred Princeton University, a private institution, from enforcing too stringent a rule on speech. Princeton had required all persons uncon-nected with the university to obtain permission before distributing political literature on campus. This case was one of a series decided by various state supreme courts that interpreted the free speech provisions of their re-spective *state* constitutions to give citizens more speech rights than are guaranteed by the First Amendment to the U.S. Constitution. Such decisions have obvious impli-cations for free speech on the campuses of state universi-ties. Some states, however, also have statutes that limit the right of private associations—in our case, private col-leges and universities—to restrict the free speech of their members. Other states have civil rights laws that protect citizens' speech beyond the protection afforded by state or federal constitutional provisions.

If you attend a private, non-religious institution in California, you should be advised that California's "Leon-ard Law" (named after its sponsoring legislator) grants students at secular private universities the same speech rights that the First Amendment and the California Con-stitution guarantee to students at public universities. This statute, passed in 1992, was the basis for a state court's declaration that a code prohibiting "offensive speech" at Stanford University, a private university, was illegal.

If you face charges that relate in any way to speech, you should find out if your state constitution or statutes establish such a right to free speech. If your state offers such protections, you may want to defend yourself by going on the offense about your protected speech rights.

Contact FIRE as soon as possible, and consult FIRE's *Guide to Free Speech on Campus* for more information on your expressive rights.

Sexual Harassment and Sexual Assault Cases at Private Colleges

All educational institutions that receive federal funding—virtually all colleges and universities, both public and private—have special legal obligations when dealing with complaints of sexual harassment and sexual assault. These obligations are discussed in greater detail in Part V, but because they bind both public *and* private colleges, it is important to introduce them here.

Title IX of the Education Amendments of 1972 states, "No person in the United States shall, on the basis of sex, be excluded from participation in, be denied the benefits of, or be subjected to discrimination under any education program or activity receiving Federal financial assistance." Federal regulations interpreting Title IX mandate that educational institutions receiving federal funding must establish "prompt and equitable" grievance procedures to hear and resolve complaints of sex discrimination. In the years since Title IX's passage, both courts and the Department of Education's Office for Civil Rights (OCR), the federal agency responsible for enforcing Title IX and other federal anti-discrimination statutes, have interpreted "discrimination" to include sexual harassment and sexual assault. As a result, the Title IX

regulatory requirement of "prompt and equitable" grievance procedures applies both to complaints about sexual
discrimination by an institution and complaints against
particular students, faculty, administrators, or staff for
sexual harassment and sexual assault.

Under Title IX, colleges and universities must prohibit discriminatory harassment that creates a "hostile
environment." As decided by the Supreme Court of the
United States in *Davis v. Monroe County Board of Education* (1999), hostile environment harassment for which a
college may be held liable occurs in the educational setting when a student is subject to targeted, unwelcome
conduct "so severe, pervasive, and objectively offensive,
and that so undermines and detracts from the victims'
educational experience, that the victim-students are effectively denied equal access to an institution's resources
and opportunities." If a college learns of hostile environment harassment, it must take action "reasonably calculated" to eliminate it and prevent its recurrence.

Title IX gives victims of sexual discrimination an interest in due process. If a student makes an allegation
of sexual assault or harassment, his or her university
must pursue the alleged perpetrator in a manner that
is "prompt and equitable." If the university does not do
so, the student can file a complaint with OCR, which
will review the university's handling of the case. If OCR
finds that there has been unfair treatment, it may take
corrective action. Title IX and its implementing regulations empower OCR to begin proceedings to strip federal
funding from a university—potentially a death blow for
all but the wealthiest institutions—so administrators

generally take compliance with Title IX very seriously.

Title IX's mandate of a "prompt and equitable" hearing in order for the *victim* to seek vindication should ensure—at least in theory—fair treatment for the *accused* as well. After all, an "equitable" procedure by definition must be a fair one. The requirement of fair procedures confers rights upon both parties in claims of sexual harassment or assault, and OCR has made clear that rights afforded to the complainant must also be afforded to the accused, and vice-versa. Of course, accused students must be presumed innocent until proven otherwise. Students and their advocates would do well to point this out in cases where they are accused of sexual misconduct. How could a process not fair to *all* parties in a case actually be "equitable"?

However, this area of the law is in dramatic flux. Unfortunately, changes to OCR's interpretation of Title IX and recent legislative initiatives regarding campus sexual harassment and sexual assault have sharply reduced the due process protections that both public and private colleges may grant students accused of such misconduct. These threats to due process are covered in more detail in Part V of this *Guide*, which focuses specifically on procedures governing sexual harassment and sexual assault.

Due Process at Religious Institutions

If you are considering attending a religious institution, you should review its code carefully to see if you are willing to be bound by it. Some religious institutions—seminaries, colleges, or universities that are associated with churches, synagogues, or mosques, for example—have strict rules governing student conduct. Private colleges are allowed to establish such rules, as long as their regulations do not violate anti-discrimination laws or other statutes.

Even then, some religiously required practices that may appear to be discriminatory—above all, in areas of sexuality—may be constitutionally protected as "the free exercise of religion." For example, rules mandating the expulsion of sexually active students by sectarian institutions are lawful, as are rules dismissing students for lacking "Christian character." In the case of *Carr v. St. John's University* (1962), the Court of Appeals of New York (the state's highest court) found no fault with the decision of St. John's University, a Catholic institution, to dismiss a student couple who married in a civil but not in a religious ceremony.

St. John's has since changed its rule that "in conformity with the ideals of Christian ... conduct, the University reserves the right to dismiss a student at any time on whatever grounds." But such a regulation would still be lawful. This is because the First Amendment's religious liberty clause, applied to the states by the Fourteenth Amendment, provides considerable autonomy to religious institutions. While not every religious practice enjoys constitutional protection (human sacrifice and the use of sacramental illegal drugs do not, for example), many practices involving adherence to religious doctrine and the freedom to associate with others of similar beliefs are protected.

Again: If you are considering attending a religious institution, you should review its code carefully to see if you are willing to be bound by it.

PART IV: DUE PROCESS IN PRACTICE

SECTION I: THE CHARGE

Notice

At public universities, due process requires that students facing suspension or expulsion for disciplinary reasons be given notice of the charges against them. What's more, due process requires that students receive this notice *before* being heard on those charges. At a *minimum*, your university must tell you both that a disciplinary action is pending against you and the charge that you face. The description of the charge should state the rule that you are accused of violating, and should describe, at least briefly, the specific act or acts that allegedly violated the rule.

That notice is required for cases involving possible suspension or expulsion from public universities was established by *Goss v. Lopez*, the landmark Supreme Court case on student discipline first discussed in Part II. As the United States Court of Appeals for the Eleventh Circuit put it in *Nash v. Auburn University* (1987), "There are no hard and fast rules by which to measure meaningful notice." But, quoting the Supreme Court, the Eleventh Circuit also noted in *Nash* that students are entitled to notice that is "reasonably calculated, under all the circumstances, to apprise [them] of the pendency of the action and afford them an opportunity to present their objections." In other words, students must be informed about the disciplinary action that they face and they must be permitted to challenge the charges against them.

DEFINITION: NOTICE

A formal announcement, notification, or warning.
—AMERICAN HERITAGE DICTIONARY

The timing and content of the notice required varies according to the circumstances. For less serious misconduct, notice may be given immediately before an informal give-and-take between student and administrator. Because the misconduct at issue is less serious—and the stakes are lower—the constitutional requirement of due process is satisfied if students are told of the charges before being asked to affirm or deny them.

More serious charges warrant more robust notice.

Following *Goss*, in which the Supreme Court noted that "[l]onger suspensions or expulsions for the remainder of the school term, or permanently, may require more formal procedures," courts have suggested that greater requirements with respect to the timing and substance of notice may be appropriate in cases that are factually complex or that present the possibility of more severe punishment. In *Flaim v. Medical College of Ohio* (2005), the United States Court of Appeals for the Sixth Circuit observed that the "stronger the private interest" in avoiding an unjust outcome, "the more likely a formal written notice—informing the accused of the charge, the policies or regulations the accused is charged with violating, and a list of possible penalties—is constitutionally required." The *Flaim* court suggested, for example, that "where factual issues are disputed, notice might also be required to include the names of witnesses and a list of other evidence the school intends to present."

But while committed to requiring meaningful notice in theory, too often courts unfortunately find almost *any* notice sufficient in practice. The courts have found in many circumstances that universities failed to live up to *Goss*'s requirement of increasingly formal hearings for increasingly serious charges (see Part IV: Section II). They have not dealt similarly, however, with the issue of more thorough or timely notice. For the courts, notice would have to be extraordinarily inadequate to be viewed as violating a student's right to due process. While late or scant notification may in fact deny a student the opportunity to mount the best possible defense, courts basically care only about whether a student is actually deprived of a meaningful opportunity to be heard—and due process arguably doesn't require much more. Nonetheless, the commitment to appropriate notice is there in court decisions, so you certainly should stake a claim to fairness in that regard.

While your university may be legally required to provide you only with basic notice a short time before your disciplinary proceeding begins, you should fight for timely, detailed notice. Sufficient time and reasonable detail about the nature of the evidence against you are crucial to the preparation of an effective defense. Many institutions provide greater notice than the law requires, so be sure to check your college's policies to see what they promise to provide.

If your school's notice does not give you the information or time you need, a simple request in writing appealing to fairness and common sense may get it for you. Be sure to lodge a formal written objection if the university sets a hearing sooner than you are ready to appear, fails to provide you with the charges against you, unexpectedly changes the charges against you before or during the hearing, or fails to tell you exactly what you did that prompted the charges. Before your hearing, write a letter stating the reasons why you cannot prepare in the time allowed and documenting the lack of detail in the notice you were provided. Getting your complaints about the notice you were provided "on the record" prior to the hearing will preserve your right to claim lack of notice in a campus appeal or in a lawsuit. Remember, speaking out about your rights and fundamental fairness may persuade the university to give you the kind of notice you need and deserve.

Preliminary Screenings

Fair and decent systems of justice do not proceed directly from what might be wild or baseless accusations to a formal hearing on serious charges. In the criminal justice system, preliminary screenings in the form of grand jury investigations or what are known as "probable cause" hearings before a judge are generally required before charges are issued. Unfortunately, campus judicial systems are not always fair and decent, and as described in Part II, campus courts are not held to the same strict standards as the criminal justice system. Nothing compels university administrators to screen out obviously unfounded cases prior to formal hearing.

Happily, some universities *do* provide for a preliminary investigation before formal charges are filed. This makes sense not only for fairness's sake, but for the sake of efficiency as well. Having a hearing can be time-consuming for all involved, including administrators, so preliminary investigations that screen out baseless accusations perform a valuable service. So while courts have generally not found a legal right to a preliminary screening before a disciplinary action can be heard, your college or university may have chosen to offer such a screening as part of its own rules. If your campus does not require such a commonsense practice, it would be good to argue on behalf of such a decent and rational change. But remember: Anything you say in a preliminary screening, no matter how informal, may be used by administrators throughout the disciplinary process.

Deferring a Campus Case When There Is a Criminal Prosecution

If you have both a university disciplinary hearing and a criminal trial pending, you will almost always want to have your disciplinary hearing postponed until *after* the criminal matter is settled. Holding the disciplinary hearing *before* the criminal trial can be very dangerous, because what you say at the campus hearing—where you have far fewer protections than in a court of law—can be used against you in the criminal case. Courts have held, however, that due process does not require campus disciplinary proceedings to be postponed until related criminal matters are settled. Further, with regard to sexual assault charges, the Department of Education's Office for Civil Rights (OCR) has stated that colleges "should not wait for the conclusion of a criminal investigation or criminal proceeding" to begin their own investigation and fact-finding, though it may delay temporarily if law enforcement is gathering evidence.

Securing a delay in your university proceeding is by

no means guaranteed. In *Goldberg v. Regents of the University of California* (1967), a California Court of Appeal sharply proclaimed that it "cannot accept the contention that where certain conduct is violative of both the rules and regulations of the University and the statutes of the state that the discipline imposed by the academic community must wait the outcome of the other proceedings."

However, some universities allow students to ask to postpone campus disciplinary proceedings until the conclusion of related criminal prosecutions. Under the University of Michigan's *Statement of Student Rights and Responsibilities*, for example, "a student undergoing civil or criminal action for the same behavior which forms the basis of a complaint ... may request a reasonable delay of the Statement resolution process until external proceedings are resolved." If your university allows for such a request, you may well want to make it. Even if your institution does *not* allow for such a request, you should consider making one, keeping in mind that there is no obligation for the institution to grant it. It is worth the effort to remind the institution of the unfairness that you would experience in the absence of such a postponement—such as not being able to fully defend yourself due to the risk of your statements being used against you in court—and the college can't agree if you don't ask.

Note, however, that if you are convicted in the criminal case, the university will frequently find you guilty of the corresponding student disciplinary charge automatically, on the basis of the criminal conviction. The theory here is that since the standard of proof is so much more stringent in the criminal court, a conviction there means that there was more than sufficient evidence to support the campus charge.

Note, too, that in sexual assault cases, the federal government requires colleges to proceed without waiting for the criminal justice system to determine guilt or innocence on charges stemming from the same conduct. As explained in more detail in Part V, OCR has issued special mandates for how colleges and universities that accept federal funding—virtually all of them—must handle sexual assault allegations. One of those special mandates prohibits delays in campus proceedings while criminal investigations are ongoing. As OCR explained in a 2011 "Dear Colleague" letter: "Schools should not wait for the conclusion of a criminal investigation or criminal proceeding to begin their own Title IX investigation and, if needed, must take immediate steps to protect the student in the educational setting." To be absolutely clear, OCR states: "For example, a school should not delay conducting its own investigation or taking steps to protect the complainant because it wants to see whether the alleged perpetrator will be found guilty of a crime." (However, as noted above, OCR does recognize that "while the police are gathering evidence," a school may need to delay its own investigation.) As a result, students facing both campus and criminal sexual assault allegations should not expect their college or university to postpone their own proceedings until the criminal justice system procedures have concluded.

For allegations not implicating Title IX, you should be aware that acquittal in the criminal court does not always mean that the campus tribunal will acquit, since the level of proof needed to convict you on campus is so much less than in a criminal trial. Still, there is considerable advantage to having the criminal trial happen first. For one thing, in a criminal trial, you will have an opportunity to fully survey the evidence against you, since you are guaranteed highly effective due process—that is, procedural and substantive safeguards of your rights as someone presumed innocent—in a criminal court.

Relatedly, success in a "probable cause" hearing conducted by the criminal justice system may help you earn an acquittal in the campus proceeding. A probable cause hearing is a preliminary proceeding conducted prior to the bringing of a formal charge on which one then would stand trial. If "probable cause" is found, you are then formally charged and put to trial. If the prosecution is unable to prove that they have probable cause to try you, the failure to meet even this very low standard should signal to the campus tribunal that its case against you is likewise too weak to proceed to a hearing on the merits of the charge. Where no probable cause to proceed is found by the criminal justice system, the university cannot credibly argue that it can find you guilty, even under the comparable (and arguably higher) "preponderance of the evidence" standard discussed in greater detail below.

If your college insists that you proceed with your campus disciplinary tribunal before your criminal trial is held, *it is essential that you retain a lawyer*. At the very least, you need legal advice about how to prevent having what you say in the campus tribunal from being used against you at a subsequent criminal trial.

Automatic Discipline After Criminal Convictions

Courts have not often considered whether students can be automatically suspended or expelled from public colleges and universities for criminal convictions. In *Paine v. Board of Regents of the University of Texas System* (1972), the U.S. District Court for the Western District of Texas held that a University of Texas rule providing for automatic suspension or expulsion of students convicted of drug offenses violated procedural due process. The court based its decision on the fact that the criminal justice system and university discipline systems serve different interests.

Statutes of Limitations

LATE CHARGES

Rules that set specific statutes of limitations—that is, time limits on charges being filed for a given act—ensure that cases will be considered while relevant witnesses are still available and memories are still fresh. Despite this obvious value, courts have not required universities to set a statute of limitations for campus disciplinary cases. The amount of due process required in administrative judicial systems is, after all, substantially different from that required in the criminal justice system. Do not count on common sense to prevail in this matter.

DEFINITION: STATUTE OF LIMITATIONS

A time limit on legal action.

—AMERICAN HERITAGE DICTIONARY

COMPLETION OF ACADEMIC REQUIREMENTS

The fact that you have completed your graduation requirements does not give you immunity from most institutions' disciplinary rules. Most universities state that the awarding of a degree is contingent not only on the completion of academic requirements but also on full compliance with the university's regulations throughout your entire time enrolled, including the period between the completion of academic requirements and graduation. Where precisely the line is drawn remains unclear.

For example, *Harwood v. Johns Hopkins University* (2000) concerned a student who shot and killed a fellow student in the time between the completion of his academic requirements and graduation exercises in 1996. The Court of Special Appeals of Maryland ruled that the university had good cause to dismiss him without a degree. As the court put it, it didn't matter that the student "would have been awarded his degree before he murdered another student if JHU had a December graduation ceremony. Rather, the critical factor is that he had yet to be awarded his degree and remained subject to the policies and procedures enumerated in the Handbook."

It is best to stay out of even far less serious trouble in the final days before the awarding of your degree.

REVOCATION OF DEGREES FROM ALUMNI

Universities appear to have the authority to revoke degrees from alumni if discoveries are made, after graduation, about the graduates' activities while they were still students. However, because of the extreme nature of revoking a degree, and the obvious damage done by such an act, universities must offer a high degree of procedural fairness in such cases.

This unusual issue arises most frequently when universities discover that students who had not in fact completed academic requirements were allowed to graduate as a result of gross error or deliberate fraud. In such cases, courts have found a justification for degree revocation in contract law: By the university's contract with the student, the degree was awarded only because of the fulfillment of certain academic requirements. If these requirements were in fact *not* fulfilled, no degree should have been issued, and the degree can therefore be revoked.

While hearings are not usually required in academic cases at public universities (see Part II), they are required in cases where degrees are going to be revoked.

This is because taking away a degree already granted is thought to be more serious than deciding not to award a degree in the first place. For example, in *Waliga v. Board of Trustees of Kent State University* (1986), the Supreme Court of Ohio ruled that once granted a degree, a graduate "possesses a property right in and to his degree" which "cannot be taken away 'except pursuant to constitutionally adequate procedures.'" Contract law also likely binds private universities to offer procedural fairness in degree revocations.

Additionally, degrees may be revoked when a university discovers after a student's graduation that he or she committed a serious disciplinary infraction while a student. For example, *Goodreau v. Rector and Visitors of the University of Virginia* (2000) concerned a university's claim to have discovered that a recent graduate had embezzled funds from a student club when still a student. The U.S. District Court for the Western District of Virginia found no legal problem with the revocation of a degree in such a case. However, in this specific instance, it refused to dismiss the student's lawsuit, finding that the university might have denied his due process rights by departing from prior assurances the student alleged receiving from officials about being able to keep his degree. The suit was settled before the court had an opportunity to explore the issue further.

Likewise, in *Jaber v. Wayne State University Board of Governors* (2011), the U.S. District Court for the Eastern District of Michigan rejected a due process claim filed by a student whose doctorate had been revoked following a plagiarism accusation. The court found that Wayne State University had provided the student with a satisfactory degree of procedural due process after a dean "held a conference, heard evidence, and made findings." The conference was informal, but the student herself chose the informal hearing over a more formal proceeding. Even the informal proceeding provided the accused student "the right to call witnesses and to be assisted by an attorney or representative." All in all, even given the high stakes, the court found that the student was afforded a "constitutionally sufficient opportunity to be heard."

Although a university may have the right to revoke your degree after graduation for misconduct in your student days, it cannot reasonably punish you for misconduct that you engaged in *after* graduation, barring a specific rule providing otherwise. The university's power must have some limits.

WITHHOLDING OF DEGREES OR SUSPENSION PENDING A HEARING

Universities sometimes suspend students from the moment that charges are brought until the completion of the disciplinary hearing. Some also withhold degrees from seniors who have completed graduation requirements but have pending disciplinary hearings—for example, when a hearing is postponed until after a criminal trial.

Temporary Suspensions

Temporary suspensions are allowed only when a student poses an immediate danger to persons or property. A hearing regarding the temporary suspension must be held as soon as practicable.

The Supreme Court explicitly stated in *Goss v. Lopez* that due process allows immediate temporary suspension without a hearing if the student poses an *immediate danger* to people or property. In short, a student accused of a violent assault could be suspended pending a hearing, but a student accused of plagiarism could not. The main purpose of the temporary suspension must be to maintain safety. Although any suspension necessarily has a punitive impact, the primary purpose of a temporary suspension cannot be to punish.

Hearings must be held for such preliminary temporary suspensions. When it is impossible or unreasonably difficult to conduct a preliminary hearing, students may be suspended immediately provided that a temporary suspension hearing is held as soon as possible. When emergency circumstances do not exist, the temporary suspension hearing must be held before the temporary suspension is put into effect.

As the amount of due process required varies with the seriousness of the possible sanction, only minimal protections are necessary at temporary suspension hearings. In the case of short preliminary suspensions, your university must give you nothing more than an opportunity to be heard. You can use this opportunity to argue that you do not pose a threat to safety, or that the temporary suspension has a punitive purpose. Universities at such hearings may not be required to consider detailed arguments about why you are innocent, except in cases of obvious error such as mistaken identity. The purpose of such a hearing is to determine if your presence on campus—before your later hearing on the actual charges against you—poses a danger. For longer preliminary suspensions or for longer periods of withholding your degree, the university may be required to meet higher standards of due process.

THREAT OF HARM TO OTHERS

Temporary suspensions may involve allegations of a student's threat of harm to others on campus. If these threats involve mental impairment, then an institution's response will be informed by the legal framework that governs college and university decision-making about students with disabilities. Title II of the Americans with Disabilities Act and Section 504 of the Rehabilitation Act of 1973, enforced by the Department of Education's Office for Civil Rights (OCR), prohibit discrimination against students on the basis of disability. (Section 504 applies to all institutions accepting federal funding, both public and private, while Title II applies only to public institutions.)

Per OCR's interpretation of Section 504's "direct threat" standard, a college or university may take "adverse action"—including suspension—against a student with a disability if he or she presents a "significant risk" to the health or safety of other campus community members. A college may determine a student presents a direct threat by conducting an individualized assessment of the student that takes into account the "nature, duration, and severity of the risk; the probability that the potential injury will actually occur; and whether reasonable modifications of policies, practices, or procedures will significantly mitigate the risk." If a college finds that a student does pose a direct threat, it may condition his or her return on the student's ability to document that he or she has met certain conditions, which may include adhering to a plan of treatment or granting the college the right to talk to his or her doctors.

Temporary suspensions may be imposed prior to providing the allegedly threatening student full due process rights when safety is at risk. As OCR wrote in a 2004 findings letter to Bluffton University: "In exceptional circumstances, such as situations where safety is of immediate concern, a college may take interim steps pending a final decision regarding adverse action against a student as long as minimal due process (such as notice and an initial opportunity to address the evidence) is provided in the interim and full due process (including a hearing and the right to appeal) is offered later."

It is vital to emphasize that, without more, an administrator's simple claim that a student presents a threat is insufficient to justify a removal from campus. Nor does an administrator's unreasonable or unsubstantiated fear of a threat allow for a temporary suspension. In *Barnes v. Zaccari* (2012), the U.S. Court of Appeals for the Eleventh Circuit found that a university president's decision to "administratively withdraw" a student deemed a threat violated the student's due process rights. Reviewing the president's belief that the student presented a "clear and present danger" to the Valdosta State University campus, the Eleventh Circuit found that "no emergency existed" to justify the removal and that in fact, the evidence "suggest[ed] that any fear was unreasonable." Because the student was denied notice and an opportunity to respond before being withdrawn, in violation of his clearly established constitutional right to due process, the Eleventh Circuit found that the president could be held personally liable for damages. On remand, a federal jury awarded the student $50,000. (FIRE helped the student find counsel and filed a "friend of the court" brief with the Eleventh Circuit urging this result.)

If you have a disability and feel as though you have suffered adverse action despite not posing a threat of harm, you should file a complaint with the Department of Education's Office for Civil Rights.

Vague Rules

Due process requires that rules must be written with enough clarity that individuals have fair warning about prohibited conduct and that police and courts have clear standards for enforcing the law without arbitrariness. Without a prohibition of vague rules, life would be a nightmare of uncertainty about what one could or could not do. The courts do not demand perfect precision in the formulation of rules, but they can find a law "void for vagueness" if people of common intelligence would have to guess at its meaning or would easily disagree about its application. For example, a rule prohibiting "bad conduct" would surely be declared void for vagueness. Who decides what is sufficiently "bad" to warrant punishment?

For the courts, how much clarity is required depends on the extent to which constitutional rights and values are involved. To punish people for conduct that they could not reasonably be expected to know or guess was prohibited raises obvious constitutional concerns, so courts insist that the criminal laws be written with the utmost clarity. Likewise, rules related to First Amendment freedoms must be wholly clear to avoid "chilling" free speech.

The courts permit codes that do not directly involve constitutionally protected matters to be written more loosely. For example, ordinary business regulations are not held to the same exacting standard as regulations affecting freedom of the press.

THE FIRST AMENDMENT AND THE "CHILLING EFFECT"

The First Amendment to the United States Constitution provides that "Congress shall make no law ... abridging the freedom of speech, or of the press; or the right of the people peaceably to assemble." This rule—that everyone can express himself or herself without undue government interference—is a cornerstone of our liberty and of our democracy.

In free speech cases, the courts have been very careful not to permit any rule that could leave unclear what speech one may or may not utter—a rule prohibiting "bad speech," for example. If individuals are afraid to speak their minds because of the possibility that their speech may be found to be illegal, they will likely refrain from speaking at all. Their speech would be "chilled"—that is, diminished and stifled. Preventing this "chilling effect" so that free people may speak their minds without fear is one of the essential goals of the First Amendment. For more on the constitutional prohibition against vague codes in the context of sexual harassment regulations, see Part V.

Courts generally have agreed that disciplinary rules at public colleges and universities do not have to be painstakingly specific when those rules do not concern constitutional protections. As a representative example, the U.S. Court of Appeals for the Third Circuit held in *Sill v.*

Pennsylvania State University (1972) that codes of conduct that are "so vague as to require speculation" violate the Fourteenth Amendment's guarantee of due process—but it simultaneously noted that codes of conduct are "not required to satisfy the same rigorous standards in this regard as are criminal statutes" because "student discipline is not analogous to criminal prosecution."

Disciplinary rules that *might* relate to speech—such as rules punishing disorderly protesters—are held to a higher standard. For example, in the 1969 case of *Soglin v. Kauffman*, the U.S. Court of Appeals for the Seventh Circuit threw out, on grounds of vagueness, the campus conviction of several students for the general crime of "misconduct." The court held that it was unclear whether the students' purposeful blocking of doorways was prohibited under the rule because the rule "contains no clues which could assist a student, an administrator or a reviewing judge in determining whether conduct not transgressing statutes is susceptible to punishment." If you are charged with violating a vague campus rule, a lawsuit could defeat the charge if you could show that the rule implicates constitutional protections.

If your case does not touch on free speech issues (or other significant constitutional interests), however, you would need evidence of a significant abuse to get a university rule voided for vagueness. Courts have upheld general campus rules in a wide range of cases. Further, if you did something *obviously* prohibited even by the vague language of the applicable rule, you usually cannot get your conviction struck down merely because there might be questions about whether *other* conduct is prohibited by the rule. For example, in *Woodis v. Westark Community College* (1998), the U.S. Court of Appeals for the Eighth Circuit found that a criminal conviction for falsifying a drug prescription was enough to violate a college rule requiring that students display "good citizenship" and "conduct themselves in an appropriate manner." The rule was admittedly vague, but despite its inadequacies, it was clear enough that the conduct—for which the student was convicted in criminal court—was covered. The more obviously criminal your conduct is at a college or university, the more likely a court will be to rule that it violated even the vaguest of prohibitions.

Private universities are not bound by constitutional prohibitions against vagueness. However, as described in Part III, courts may give students the benefit of the doubt in interpreting the handbooks of private universities, because students have no say in writing the rules. You can use the vagueness of a private university's rules to your advantage in defending against a disciplinary charge by arguing that your institution did not give you reasonable grounds to know that your conduct was prohibited.

Overbroad Rules

Laws are said to be *overbroad* if, in addition to whatever else they prohibit, they restrict protected First Amendment freedoms. The overbreadth doctrine has its roots not in the due process clause, but in the First Amendment's guarantees of freedom of speech, assembly, and press. However, when a provision of a law violates the First Amendment, it is possible to salvage the rest of the law by removing the offending section. A law prohibiting physically assaulting and criticizing an official would be successfully challenged—but a court would likely remove the ban on criticism, not the ban on physical assault. Laws themselves can only be ruled overbroad if they make it impossible to separate their constitutional and unconstitutional provisions without writing a completely new law.

Laws can be vague without being overbroad, but vagueness often contributes to a finding of overbreadth. For example, in *Soglin v. Kauffman* (1969), discussed above, the Seventh Circuit found the university's ban on "misconduct" to be not only vague, but also so overbroad that it allowed the university to punish any conduct it wished, including conduct protected by the First Amendment. The policy's use of the term "misconduct" was found to be vague because reasonable people can easily differ about what was prohibited. With a term this vague, campus police and university administrators could charge students for doing anything that personally offended the officer or administrator, giving officials arbitrary, unlimited power. The policy's use of "misconduct" was also found *overbroad*, because the term would stop people from engaging in a wide variety of ordinary activities out of fear of doing something improper.

Because public universities have less leeway on free speech protections, you may have a stronger case than you might imagine against an overbroad campus rule.

Unfair Rules

Public universities possess significant authority to prevent disruptions of the educational process. However, this authority does not give public universities the right to enact rules unrelated to legitimate institutional objectives. It does not give them the right to create rules that are arbitrary or grossly unfair, that violate the First Amendment or other constitutional rights, or that intrude unnecessarily upon the rights of privacy or conscience. At a *public* university, you can successfully challenge disciplinary proceedings that are based on an unconstitutional rule.

Public universities are prohibited from establishing rules that infringe on students' rights to make certain individual choices. For example, public universities may not punish students under strict regulations regarding dress and hairstyle. In *Reichenberg v. Nelson* (1970), the U.S. District Court for the District of Nebraska found that Chadron State College's requirement that male students be clean-shaven was unreasonable because the institution "cannot refuse entrance to one in all other respects qualified because he chooses to exercise his constitutional rights." While public *high schools* may be allowed to restrict students' personal appearance to some extent, public *colleges and universities*—whose students are overwhelmingly adults—may make only the narrowest regulations essential to a reasonable and permissible goal.

Keep in mind that while private colleges may not make utterly arbitrary rules, they do have the right, as private associations, to regulate much more conduct than public universities, as long as students agree to be governed by those regulations in matriculating. Private colleges are limited by the rules of civilized society, however. They may not commit fraud in attracting students—advertising one thing but delivering another—and they may not violate their contracts or otherwise break the law.

FIRE publishes *Guides* dealing with some of the serious violations of substantive rights common to many contemporary colleges and universities. You will likely benefit by consulting FIRE's other *Guides* when preparing to defend yourself against disciplinary charges brought on the basis of conduct that is in fact protected by the First Amendment or by substantive due process. Do not let our emphasis on procedural due process in this *Guide* distract you from the substantive defense that you must offer if you are charged with conduct that should not be an offense in the first place.

"CONDUCT UNBECOMING A STUDENT"

Some institutions of higher education have rules that prohibit students from engaging in "misconduct," "dishonorable conduct," or "conduct unbecoming a student." These rules all have potential constitutional weaknesses at public institutions.

As discussed above, a rule prohibiting unspecified misconduct is almost certainly unconstitutional because it is impermissibly vague, offering virtually no useful guidance as to what conduct is prohibited. A rule prohibiting "dishonorable conduct" is less vague, because it specifies the conduct that is not allowed—namely, conduct that lacks honor. But such a rule is still probably unconstitutionally overbroad, because much conduct protected by the First Amendment lacks "honor" in some observer's estimation. It is dishonorable to speak meanly to or about your mother, but you have a First Amendment right to be mean in speech (as long as your speech does not cross over into some prohibited category—by including threats of physical violence, for example).

Otherwise broad and vague "conduct unbecoming" rules may be acceptable for professions or trades with generally established and understood standards of conduct. For example, the standards of conduct for professionals such as doctors, members of the military, and judges are so long established, widely known, and generally accepted that these standards of conduct may not need to be spelled out in writing. In sharp contrast, students—even students in professional schools—are not yet part of a profession or trade and do not share such generally accepted responsibilities. Norms of conduct vary widely between different types of universities and areas of the country, and, indeed, the history of student life has been one of constant challenges and changes to such norms.

"PROFESSIONALISM" AS SPEECH CODE

In recent years, FIRE has witnessed a disturbing growth in incidents of public college students punished for failing to abide by general "professionalism" codes. In effect, administrators have begun using "professionalism" as a general catch-all provision to punish dissenting, unpopular, or simply unwanted student speech that they would otherwise be constitutionally prohibited from punishing.

FIRE made this point in a 2013 *amicus curiae* ("friend of the court") brief submitted with the Student Law Press Center to the U.S. Court of Appeals for the Ninth Circuit in the case of *Oyama v. University of Hawaii*. The student brought suit against the university after he was expelled from its teacher education program for expressing his views about students with disabilities and age-of-consent laws. The university deemed these views "not in alignment" with professional norms in education. As FIRE and the Student Press Law Center argued in our brief, authored by Professor Eugene Volokh:

> If universities may dismiss students from educational programs on the grounds that the student's views fail to comply with dominant professional norms, then most of these

campus speech codes could be revived merely by being slightly reworded (for instance, on the theory that allegedly bigoted or otherwise offensive speech is contrary to professional norms). Indeed, if university student speech expressing calm, reasoned views on important public policy topics such as age of consent laws and disability education policy is stripped of First Amendment protection, then universities would have a virtually free hand in engaging in the viewpoint discrimination that the Supreme Court has long condemned.

FIRE and the SPLC pointed out that while law professors might think an anarchist student would be a poor lawyer, or that psychiatric professors in the 1960s might have thought that a student who believed that homosexuality was normal was "not in alignment" with the norms of the profession, expelling students for these views would not only be unconstitutional but also would harm the professions themselves. Enforcing professional standards on students would cause the professions to stagnate, as students with unconventional or controversial views are refused entry.

In addition to the First Amendment problems presented by the use of "professionalism" codes to silence students, such codes present due process problems, as well. Because students—who, after all, are not *yet* members of a profession—do not possess the professional knowledge to accurately determine what "professional norms" may and may not prohibit, they will rationally choose to stay silent to avoid punishment. This "chilling effect," promulgated by the vagueness of the "professionalism" requirement, violates students' rights both to speak their minds and to receive proper notice of the boundaries of acceptable conduct.

Infractions Committed Off Campus

Public universities may discipline students for their conduct off campus, even if the conduct at issue has little to do with university life. Private universities may extend their jurisdiction beyond the bounds of campus, too, if they notify students in published materials that they do so. For example, in *Ray v. Wilmington College* (1995), an Ohio Court of Appeals noted that "[a]n educational institution's authority to discipline its students does not necessarily stop at the physical boundaries of the institution's premises." Rather, the court found that "[t]he institution has the prerogative to decide that certain types of off-campus conduct are detrimental to the institution and to discipline a student who engages in that conduct."

Although colleges and universities may discipline students for a wide range of behaviors occurring off campus, some universities have policies that restrict their own disciplinary jurisdiction. Don't get too comfortable, however, if your school's handbook limits discipline to offenses "detrimental to the university" or "adversely affecting the interests of the college." Such phrases can be interpreted to cover off-campus offenses that don't involve other students. Some universities specifically restrict off-campus discipline to offenses that affect other students. If this is the case at your university, you may have a strong claim that the institution may not punish you for your off-campus conduct with regard to nonstudents, because, as noted repeatedly, schools must follow their own rules.

CHARGES THAT THREATEN FREE SPEECH

The due process to which you are entitled in a university disciplinary hearing varies by the circumstances of your case. Because First Amendment rights are so sacred, courts often hold that a greater amount of process is due in cases that involve freedom of speech, assembly, and the press. For example, rules and regulations must be clearer and more specific. If your case has First Amendment implications, it is always a good idea to highlight these in order to support your argument for a higher level of due process. Even from a strictly tactical perspective, when you are able to defend yourself on free speech grounds, you almost always find yourself fighting from higher moral ground than would otherwise be the case. Students defending themselves in cases that involve speech issues should consult FIRE's *Guide to Free Speech on Campus*.

When Student Groups Face Charges

University authority to punish student groups was acknowledged by the Supreme Court of the United States in *Healy v. James* (1972). Although the Court offered few clues about exactly what steps must be followed in disciplinary proceedings for student groups, it did suggest that any adverse action taken against a group be based on substantial evidence and not mere speculation. Because due process is flexible, precisely what procedures are required depends on the particular circumstances. As a general rule, the constitutional guarantee of freedom of association gives more protection to expressive organizations, such as political clubs, than to social associations such as fraternities.

Colleges may sanction a student association that collectively engages in activities prohibited by university rules. However, the misdeeds of a few (or even of a majority) of the members of an association do not always justify disciplinary action against the association as a whole. "Guilt by association," absent other evidence, is rightly viewed as unjust. For such a collective punishment to be permissible, the group *in its totality* should have shared a prohibited intent or conspired in the commission or cover-up of misconduct. This principle should be particularly strong on a public campus where the First Amendment's protection of freedom of association must be honored. The point at which an entire group may be punished for the infractions of a few of its members is, nonetheless, a difficult matter to determine.

A prosecuted group should remind the tribunal of the injustice of guilt by association in the absence of evidence that the offending members were acting in accord with the organization's practices and policies, with the wishes or knowledge of a substantial number of members, or with the approval of the organization's leadership. The First Amendment's guarantee of freedom of association would mean little if an entire group could be prosecuted, or even disbanded, because of the unauthorized actions of a few.

Sexual Assault Charges

Sexual assault is a painful reality on campuses, as it is elsewhere in our society. Each offense is an extremely grave matter. Sexual assault is the most serious crime that comes before campus courts. (For a discussion of why colleges handle rape charges, and the lessened due process protections that students accused of sexual assault are afforded as a result of recent administrative and legislative action, please see Part V.)

If you are the victim of sexual assault on campus, you likely have significant institutional resources available to you. Colleges are perhaps more aware of the very real problem of sexual assault than other parts of society. Accordingly, colleges generally provide extensive counseling resources that may be of assistance and comfort. Under Title IX, for example, the Department of Education has made clear that you must be notified of your right to "any available resources, such as counseling, health, and mental health services," as well as your right to file a criminal complaint. Administrators should be well versed in these options.

Students facing sexual assault allegations in the campus judicial system must confront the prospect of a life-altering finding of guilt without the due process protections such high stakes would otherwise demand. College disciplinary procedures are simply not designed to handle cases involving the subtle and complex issues typically involved in sexual assault cases. Unfortunately, some campus judicial systems employ procedures that are so deficient that they cannot discriminate between meritorious and non-meritorious accusations. For example, the "preponderance of evidence" standard of proof mandated by the Office for Civil Rights is insufficient in sexual assault cases. In a pure "he-said, she-said" case, accusation alone could be judged as sufficient to meet the burden, since what the alleged victim said might be judged by itself to satisfy such a standard.

The heinousness of sexual assault can overwhelm campus judicial systems and result in guilty findings in cases lacking merit. Political considerations can sway hearing panels, especially in situations where well-meaning campus activists have publicized the case and increased pressure to secure a guilty finding. Moreover, a mere accusation in the campus system is usually sufficient to lead to a full hearing; there is usually no preliminary screening step to protect students from being hauled into a tribunal on the basis of misguided or wholly inadequate accusations.

If accused of sexual assault, you should hire an attorney and argue for the fair hearing to which you are entitled by due process. At a public university, highlighting the gravity of the charges may help get you greater procedural protections, as more serious charges require greater due process. At a private university, this is also a powerful moral argument. In a civilized society, the more serious the charge, the greater the protections that are offered to a defendant.

If you are falsely accused of rape in campus courts, be aware that a parallel criminal action is not inevitable. Because of the lack of procedural protections, university disciplinary process invites accusations that rightly would not survive the highly public criminal justice system. In a real court, you have rights to fair process and reasonable safeguards that are far more rigorous than even the best campuses offer.

Since the prosecution's burden of proof at a criminal trial is "proof beyond a reasonable doubt," campus prosecutors sometimes claim that acquittal in a court of law should not automatically require acquittal in the campus tribunal, where the level of proof needed for conviction is much lower. However, an acquittal in the criminal courts (or, as discussed above, the prosecution's failure to show "probable cause" in a preliminary hearing) can make successful campus prosecutions considerably more difficult. Universities may be reluctant to make factual findings that are different from those of other, more rigorous bodies that have considered the same case.

SECTION II: THE RECORD

Federal law requires all colleges and universities—public and private—to keep the records of student disciplinary cases confidential, but to disclose these records to the defendants upon their request.

The Family Educational Rights and Privacy Act (FERPA) of 1974 makes a student's "education records" confidential, but it gives students and their parents the right to inspect them. FERPA delineates precisely who may and may not see a student's records and under what circumstances. Your rights under FERPA are much clearer than your due process rights, which come from judicial precedent rather than statute and which vary widely by both specific case and jurisdiction. Furthermore, unlike due process, FERPA applies equally to all institutions, public or private, that receive any Department of Education funding—that is to say, virtually all colleges and universities.

For some time, there was ambiguity over the extent to which FERPA applied to disciplinary records. However, a number of cases, including the 2002 ruling of the U.S. Court of Appeals for the Sixth Circuit in *U.S. v. Miami University*, discussed later, make clear that disciplinary records are "educational records" covered by FERPA.

FERPA therefore gives you the right to inspect any and all documents about you created by the university in the course of your disciplinary case. Others may *not* examine these records. As with your transcript, the substance of your disciplinary file is confidential. The university may not share information in it, even orally, with anyone other than you and certain specific university officers and staff, unless you waive your rights to such confidentiality.

You have the right to see not only material that has been placed in your official file, but all documents about your case created by the university, no matter who created them or where they are stored. You don't have a right to see notes, however, such as the handwritten notes at meetings that individual administrators or professors made for their personal use and have not shared with others or "maintained" as part of an official record. There is no way under FERPA to access a school official's personal notes unless the official gives them to you voluntarily. (It never hurts to ask, however.) Additionally, you don't have a right to see records generated by the campus police that were not turned over to the disciplinary committee. These are considered regular police records. The police may show them to other law enforcement agencies, or to prosecutors, all subject to their normal rules. You can try to see these records under state freedom of information laws, but this is very difficult or even impossible in many jurisdictions. (Note: If you sue, you may receive access to personal notes via the "discovery" process discussed earlier.)

Access to Records

If you want to inspect the records of your disciplinary case, under FERPA, your college or university is required to gather them and give you access them to them within 45 days. Your university is not required to let you photocopy your records, and many universities do not allow students to do so. Universities are required to allow you to copy them, however, if preventing you from doing so effectively prohibits you from seeing them.

At the conclusion of your case, if your university has decided to permanently retain documents about you that you would rather see destroyed, you may ask the university to discard them. If administrators refuse to do so, you have the right to a hearing before an impartial officer of the university to ask that the materials be removed. If you can demonstrate at that hearing that the information in your file is inaccurate, misleading, or otherwise in violation of your privacy rights, the university must correct your records. The law specifically allows the university to maintain records about disciplinary actions taken against you, however, so it is unlikely that you will succeed in having your disciplinary record expunged at such a hearing. However, FERPA requires that you be allowed to place a statement in your file explaining any problems you see with any aspects of your educational records, which the university must release if, under circumstances such as a court order, it releases the records themselves.

Your college or university has the right to disclose

information about your disciplinary case to your professors or university officials if they have a "legitimate educational interest" in that information. When you apply to graduate or professional school, or seek to transfer schools, your college may forward records related to you, including information about your disciplinary record. In such a case, however, it must inform you that this is its policy or make a reasonable attempt to contact you with regard to the transmission of the records. It must also you provide you a copy of the records it released at your request.

Release of Records

If you are found responsible for violent misconduct, the Higher Education Amendments of 1998 give your university the right to report your name and the "final result" of your case to the general public. (Note that the "final result" need not necessarily be *entirely* final. The federal regulations implementing FERPA define "final result" as simply "a decision or determination, made by an honor court or council, committee, commission, or other entity authorized to resolve disciplinary matters within the institution." So even if you or your accuser have a right to appeal a panel's verdict, that panel's finding still qualifies as a "final result," per FERPA.)

If you are found responsible for violent misconduct or a sex offense in a campus proceeding, your university may disclose your name, the violation you committed, and the punishment you received to any member of the public, including the news media. Universities do not have an *obligation* under FERPA to reveal this information. They may refuse requests to divulge it. (However, at public institutions, state laws may sometimes compel disclosure of these records.) A 2014 joint survey by the Student Press Law Center and *The Columbus Dispatch* found that 25 of 110 institutions contacted provided the "final result" of disciplinary hearings concerning violent misconduct; the rest cited state laws or FERPA as prohibiting the disclosure of such records.

Even if your university chooses to speak to the press, however, it may disclose only the final result of your case, keeping the documents related to it confidential. You should note, though, that under the Clery Act of 1990 and its subsequent amendments, universities are required to make reports to the general campus community about certain very serious crimes that are reported to campus security or the local police. (See the next section for more on when universities must report crimes to the police.) The content of these reports, however, may not be such that it will violate your rights under FERPA.

If you are charged with an act of violence, your college or university *may* tell the victim whether you were found responsible. If you are charged with a sex offense, the university *must* tell the victim whether you were found responsible. The university is not allowed to tell the victim about the outcome of cases involving any violations or rules beyond these categories, such as nonviolent

95

theft.

Whether your college may tell your parents about your disciplinary case depends on the nature of the accusation, whether your parents claim you as a dependent on their tax return, and, for some types of accusations, your age. If your parents declare you as a dependent on their tax return, your college may show them all of your educational records, including your disciplinary file. Most parents declare their college-age children as dependents on their tax return, so your parents may have access to your disciplinary file.

Whether or not your parents claim you as a dependent, a university may tell your parents if you are found responsible for an offense involving drugs or alcohol, if you are under twenty-one years old at the time of disclosure. Also, as noted above, the university may tell anyone it pleases—including your parents—if you are found responsible for a violation of disciplinary rules involving violence or sex.

Within the boundaries of the law, universities may set their own policies about when to divulge disciplinary records to students' parents. Under no circumstances is a college or university *required* to tell a student's parents of the student's record. Except in the circumstances mentioned above, your university has an affirmative obligation *not* to tell your parents about the final result of your case. Thus, if you are not a dependent and are found responsible for nonviolent theft, for example, your university may not reveal this information to your parents.

Universities take their obligations under FERPA very seriously. Although you may not sue your university for improperly disclosing your records, you may file a complaint with the Department of Education's Family Policy Compliance Office (www.ed.gov/offices/OM/fpco) if you believe that your university has acted improperly on a FERPA issue. The Department of Education can cut off federal funding from universities that have a practice or policy of violating FERPA. Typically, however, individual violations of FERPA do not tend to result in significant sanctions.

RIGHT TO CONFIDENTIALITY FOR WITNESSES AND VICTIMS

Generally speaking, colleges and universities may not reveal the names of witnesses or crime victims without their written consent. However, you should be aware that certain exceptions to FERPA may apply in this context.

For example, if your university creates records about the allegations that you made or crimes that you witnessed, your parents may see them if you are declared a dependent on your parents' most recent tax return. Universities may also send reports containing the names of witnesses or crime victims to the police, prosecutors, judges, or attorneys engaged in litigation under certain circumstances. At this point, the fact that you were the victim of or witness to a crime may become available under public records laws, and may be accessible to the general public.

If a notation that you were the victim of or witness to a crime is placed in your permanent file and you do not wish it to be there, you have the right to ask your university to remove it and, if the institution refuses, you have a right to a hearing before an impartial officer of the university. The hearing officer has the power to order that your records be modified if they are inaccurate, misleading, or otherwise in violation of your privacy rights. If your record is not modified, you have the right to attach a statement to your record explaining your dissatisfaction with it.

These and other exceptions are discussed in detail in the *FERPA General Guidance for Students* issued by the Family Policy Compliance Office, available at http://www2.ed.gov/policy/gen/guid/fpco/ferpa/students.html.

Confidentiality and the Charge Against You

Federal privacy laws classify materials about your disciplinary case as educational records. Consequently, your university is obliged by FERPA to keep them confidential. (Note, however, that universities may ask their law enforcement units to investigate possible criminal activity.) If your disciplinary matter has not yet reached the police (at which point a great deal of information about it becomes a matter of public record), you may keep it confidential or decide to tell others—including, if you choose, the media—about it.

Deciding whether to publicize your case during your

investigation or hearing is a complex tactical decision. Publicity can have powerful effects on the fate of a charge and on your chances of receiving a fair determination of guilt or innocence. If there is any ambiguity about your guilt, however, you may want to avoid gaining publicity for your case. The heightened scrutiny that media focus brings may draw attention to the deficiencies of your case, and may provoke university officials to impose *more* severe sanctions because of public pressure or the effects of negative publicity. If the evidence is strongly in your favor, however, and if the administration, despite the lack of evidence or the unfairness of a charge, remains stubbornly determined to convict you, then publicity can often be very beneficial. However, if you are accused of a serious offense, the stigma of being associated with an accusation—even when false—may outweigh the benefits of publicity.

It is a serious matter for universities to release any information about your disciplinary case to the media without your consent, before, during, or after your hearing. The disciplinary committee is forbidden from revealing your name to the media, and it is similarly prohibited from leaking information describing your case without using your name. In practice, universities tend to be very careful about observing these restrictions.

In the event of a violation of federal privacy laws, you cannot personally sue your university under FERPA, but you can report the problem to the Department of Education's Family Policy Compliance Office. That office can apply a variety of sanctions against the university, including, at the most extreme, revocation of federal funding. Typically, however, colleges and universities are happy to obey FERPA's privacy and confidentiality provisions. In general, universities prefer to operate their disciplinary systems outside of the glare of publicity.

Some colleges and universities impose "gag orders" on student defendants, requiring them to stay silent about the disciplinary proceedings against them or barring them from disclosing the names of their co-defendants or accusers. Although universities sometimes claim that FERPA requires such rules, it does not. FERPA restricts disclosure only by universities, not by students. (For an obvious example, FERPA prevents *the university* from inappropriately making your grades public. That does not prevent *you* from talking or complaining about your grades.)

Using the Laws About Educational Records to Your Advantage

In preparing your defense, it may be useful to have two types of information that you can obtain under educational records laws.

In 1990, Congress passed the Campus Security Act, which modified FERPA to allow colleges and universities to inform the alleged victim of a violent crime about the results of disciplinary proceedings against the crime's alleged perpetrator. Congress modified this rule again in

1998 to include "nonforcible sex offenses," to note that only "final results" may be disclosed, and to allow for sharing this information with the public, not just the alleged victim. If you are accused of a crime of violence or a sex offense, you should request the data about other campus cases, so that you know how students previously accused of such offenses were treated.

In preparing your case, you also may be able to use your right under FERPA to inspect your educational records to your advantage. Your university must let you inspect all of your educational records—other than police records or handwritten notes—within 45 days of your request. This gives you the right to inspect materials related to your disciplinary case that may be in the college's files. Reviewing these materials would obviously be very helpful, letting you see the details of the university's case against you. If your university is unable to provide the records to you in sufficient time to prepare for your hearing, you may want to ask for a postponement until the university satisfies your pending FERPA request.

SECTION III: THE HEARING

The Right to Be Heard and to Hear the Evidence Against You

If you face suspension or expulsion from a public university, you have a right to hear the evidence against you and to have an opportunity to rebut it. This right was first recognized by the Supreme Court in *Goss v. Lopez* (1975). In that case, as discussed earlier, the Court found the suspension of high school students unconstitutional because the students had not been told of the evidence against them and had not been given a chance to respond to it. The Court held that any student facing suspension must be given "an explanation of the evidence the authorities have and an opportunity to present his side of the story."

However, the right to be heard does not necessarily extend to a right to a formal hearing—that is, a live proceeding at which evidence is taken and witnesses are called. Under *Goss*, public universities may establish any type of proceeding or mechanism that allows accused students a fair opportunity to hear the evidence against them and to tell their side of the story fully. Because a fact-finding hearing is the most logical, straightforward way to fulfill *Goss*'s requirements, however, most public universities hold hearings in serious disciplinary cases.

In fact, hearings may be required in more serious cases, because *Goss* holds that the more serious the potential punishment, the more due process protections are required. But courts have not decided with any clarity or uniformity that students have a right to a formal hearing, as they generally avoid dictating the internal proceedings of universities and permit university disciplinary proceedings to be much less elaborate than those of criminal trials.

Hearing procedures need not be the same for all offenses. Indeed, the idea that greater protections are needed for increasingly serious charges is a basic principle of due process. Even the criminal justice system dispenses with jury trials for minor offenses where the maximum penalty is very modest. Nonetheless, due process requires that similar cases be handled by similar procedures. Public universities are also obliged to treat similar cases in a similar way under the Fourteenth Amendment's guarantee of "equal protection of the laws," which requires that the government apply the same rules to people in similar circumstances. Your public university must have a very good reason indeed to handle your case differently from similar past cases. If you become aware of discrepancies between how your case and a similar case was handled—whether regarding the procedures used or the punishment received—your right to due process may have been violated, and you should register a complaint and seek legal advice.

There are some cases in which hearings are not

required. For example, if you admit your guilt to the charges against you, you waive your right to be heard on the issue of guilt versus innocence. While this may sound obvious, there are cases where students have admitted guilt and then tried to sue their universities for deprivation of due process because they were punished without a hearing. Once guilt is admitted, the need for a hearing—at least on the issue of guilt—largely disappears. For this reason, particularly when informally meeting with administrators about new disciplinary charges, you should be very careful about what you say, and err on the side of saying less rather than more. Be sure to think about this if your university tries to convince you to plead guilty to a charge of which you know you are innocent. Even if you have admitted guilt, you might still be entitled to a hearing on the issue of appropriate punishment. But if you have agreed to accept a lesser punishment in exchange for accepting responsibility, you may have waived your due process rights or right to appeal. Be very wary of such offers if you are innocent.

Similarly, if your university determines that you pose an ongoing threat of disrupting the educational process or an immediate danger of harming persons or property, you may be temporarily suspended without a hearing or notice, provided that a temporary suspension hearing is held as soon as possible. (See Part IV, Section I.)

At a private university, you do not have a legal right to a hearing—although you certainly should argue for your moral right to one—unless the university promises such a hearing to you and is bound by the principles of contract law in the university's state. Most universities, however, do promise hearings, and if the university says that it will grant you a hearing, you may be able to get a court to hold them to their word. For example, in *Tedeschi v. Wagner College* (1980), the Court of Appeals of New York ruled that an expelled student who had been granted something less than the actual hearing promised in a student handbook was entitled to reinstatement pending a new and, this time, adequate hearing.

Similarly, in *Corso v. Creighton University* (1984), the U.S. Court of Appeals for the Eighth Circuit found that Creighton University had violated its contract with a student who was expelled for cheating. The Eighth Circuit noted that the discipline stemmed from an academic matter—and courts, as we have seen, are generally loath to interfere with academic decisionmaking. Nevertheless, the Eighth Circuit found the Student Handbook's promise of a hearing in "all cases where misconduct may result in serious penalties" to be determinative, and it held that the student "must be afforded his contractual right to such a hearing prior to being expelled from the medical school."

The Right to be Present at a Formal Hearing

As established in *Goss*, you have the right to hear for yourself an "an explanation of the evidence" against you before you present your defense. As a result, if your public university uses a formal hearing to decide your case, you have the right, even where potential punishments are minimal, to be present at all of the hearing in order to hear the evidence being used against you. This protection, unlike many of the others we have discussed, applies broadly because while allowing you to be present creates only a minor burden to the university, it can have a major impact on the fairness of the proceedings.

Courts have overturned the decisions of university tribunals where the right to be present at the entirety of a formal hearing was denied. For example, in *University of Texas Medical School v. Than* (1995), the Supreme Court of Texas overturned the expulsion of a student from a public medical school because the student was not allowed to accompany the hearing officer and a school representative when they visited the site of the alleged offense. The court ordered a new hearing for the student. This has been an area where obvious notions of fairness have generally prevailed. Accordingly, most institutions expressly grant accused students the right to be present at a formal hearing. If yours does not, and you may be barred from your hearing, you should file a written notice of protest and request the right to be present.

The Accuser as Prosecutor

In the criminal justice system, the only role that the accuser plays is that of witness. Our system views crime as an offense against society rather than merely against the individual victim, and charges are brought by prosecutors as agents of "the people." At public and private universities, an arrangement in which a person reporting a disciplinary offense must personally prosecute the case against the accused student at the disciplinary hearing is perhaps legally permissible, but is still undesirable. Forcing the accuser to undertake the burdensome work of prosecuting cases deters the reporting of offenses and makes conviction dependent not on the merits of the case but on the accuser's skill.

At a public university, the accused may have a right to object to an arrangement in which the alleged victim is prosecuting the case. A prosecutor's range of choices— known as "prosecutorial discretion"— can have a profound effect on the outcome of a case. Because of that, accused persons, in the non-university context, are entitled to a prosecutor who is impartial before entering the case. Although courts have not considered the question, due process may allow accused students to prevent their accusers from being their prosecutors in the university setting. It may be more effective, however, for either the accuser or the accused, or both, to simply make a non-legal argument that it is unfair to force the accuser to take on the role of prosecutor.

The Right to Hire a Lawyer

A university may not interfere with your right to hire an attorney to assist you in preparing your case. However,

your right to benefit from the presence or active participation of an attorney in meetings or hearings may differ
depending on the type of case you are fighting and the
state in which your college is located.

If you are accused of sexual assault, the Violence
Against Women Reauthorization Act of 2013 (VAWA)
grants you the right to have the advisor of your choice—
including an attorney—present at disciplinary hearings
and all related meetings and proceedings. (The accuser
enjoys the same right, described in more detail in Part V.)
Note, however, that per Department of Education regulations, your institution may still limit your attorney's
ability to actively participate in the proceedings—for
example, by limiting his or her ability to speak on your
behalf.

If your college is part of the University of North Carolina system, you or your student organization enjoy the
right to the active participation of counsel (or, if you prefer, a non-attorney advocate) at your expense in cases
involving non-academic disciplinary charges. FIRE lobbied in support of this right, which was secured by an
overwhelmingly bipartisan vote of the state legislature
and signed into law in 2013. FIRE is actively pursuing
passage of similar laws in other states, so be sure to visit
our website, thefire.org, to see if we have been successful
in your state.

Some states have also established a right to be represented by hired counsel in all state administrative agency
proceedings. Of the states that have passed such statutory

protections, courts in three of them—Washington, Tennessee, and Oregon—have found that public college disciplinary hearings are state administrative proceedings. You may well have a right to be represented by private counsel if you go to school in those states. Courts in ten other states with an established right to counsel in administrative proceedings (Alaska, Arizona, Arkansas, California, Hawaii, Kansas, Maryland, Montana, New Hampshire, and New Mexico) have yet to rule on whether public college disciplinary hearings qualify as state administrative proceedings. If you attend school in those states, it may be worth testing your right to have an attorney present in a hearing. Again, it is important to know and use your state law.

Outside of these specific cases and states, it is important to remember that the Sixth Amendment's celebrated guarantee of the right to counsel applies only to criminal trials. In terms of campus disciplinary cases, a claim of right to counsel would have to stem from the due process clause—and most courts have agreed that due process does not require universities to allow students to bring lawyers into ordinary disciplinary proceedings, even when expulsion is at stake. For example, in *Jaksa v. Regents of the University of Michigan* (1984), the District Court for the Eastern District of Michigan declined to find that a failure to allow the defendant to be represented by counsel at a suspension hearing violated his due process rights.

However, since *Goss* does hold that greater due process

is required in more serious cases, some courts have taken this to mean that additional procedural protections such as the right to counsel are required in some special circumstances. For example, in *Gabrilowitz v. Newman* (1978), the U.S. Court of Appeals for the First Circuit held that due process requires that students be allowed to retain counsel to advise them at disciplinary hearings when related criminal charges are pending. Because such situations present complicated concerns about self-incrimination, the court held that it would be a denial of due process to force the student to proceed without a lawyer. However, the First Circuit stated that due process requires only that the lawyer be allowed in the hearing room to advise the student. The college may still ban the lawyer from making arguments and questioning witnesses.

Some courts have also held that when a university's case is presented by a lawyer or other legally experienced person, that university must allow students to retain a lawyer to represent them at the hearing, that is, to make arguments and question witnesses on their behalf. In *French v. Bashful* (1969), the U.S. District Court for the Eastern District of Louisiana overturned a disciplinary action against students at a public university because while a third-year law student presented the university's case at the hearing, the students themselves were not allowed to be represented by counsel. It stopped short, however, of ordering the university to provide free counsel for indigent students.

Outside of sexual assault hearings, in which the role of advisors is governed by VAWA as explained above, private universities may bar lawyers from their disciplinary proceedings. You nonetheless may wish to seek the advice of an attorney, even if he or she may not join you at a hearing. In fact, since most of the work on your defense will be done outside the hearing room, a lawyer can provide a great deal of help. You need to weigh the costs involved against the possible harm that you might suffer from an unjust conviction or punishment. (If your case is minor and the threat of serious punishment is low or non-existent, it may not make sense to retain counsel.) It also never hurts to ask whether you may bring your lawyer with you to your hearing. As is the case with many of the other protections we discuss, many universities are more flexible in this area than the law requires.

Composition of the Hearing Panel

A hearing before an *impartial* fact-finder and decision-maker is essential to due process. The impartiality of tribunals is one of the hallmarks of a decent society and a fundamental requirement for any chance at a just outcome. While the basic principle that the panel hearing your case must be free of bias applies to disciplinary hearings at public colleges and universities, courts nevertheless have held that certain accommodations may be made to the unique circumstances of institutions of higher education. Administrators may serve on your hearing panel, and panelists may even have had prior involvement with your case. In other words, the rules are looser than they are in the criminal or civil context. But the fundamental principles of fairness and reasonableness still apply.

Hearing boards in university disciplinary cases must be free from unreasonable bias. If you believe that the tribunal that is hearing your case is biased, you should object in writing before the panel even considers your case. Given human nature, you stand the greatest chance of having biased panelists removed *before* the panel has invested time and effort in your case. When you state your reasons for your challenge, you should be as specific as possible, placing facts, not speculations, on the record. Some institutions specifically provide the right to file such a challenge, and have established a procedure for doing so.

If the panel in your case displayed bias, you will want to raise that as a crucial issue in any formal or informal university appeal process. If all else fails, you can file, or threaten to file, a lawsuit on the basis of the panel's bias. To succeed in such a lawsuit you will need to show explicitly that a panelist approached his or her duties after having already formed an opinion regarding the charge. (This is easiest, of course, when a panelist has commented publicly on your case before the hearing.) When this standard of unacceptable conduct is reached, courts will sometimes overturn student convictions.

For example, in *Marshall v. Maguire* (1980), a New

York court vacated the expulsion of a student at a state university because one individual had served on both his hearing and appeals panels. The court concluded logically that someone who already had voted to find the student responsible at a hearing clearly had formed an opinion on the charge before serving on the appellate panel. In this case, such a denial of due process—which also violated the university's own procedures—cast a shadow on the university's entire disciplinary process. As a result, the court overturned the rulings of both the original and the appellate panels.

Likewise, in *Furey v. Temple University* (2010), the U.S. District Court for the Eastern District of Pennsylvania allowed a student's due process challenge of his expulsion from Temple University (a public institution) to proceed because of questions about the hearing panel's impartiality. The court's ruling rested in significant part on the fact that the student accused of misconduct was subjected to skeptical questioning, bordering on outright hostility, that struck a sharp contrast with the way opposing witnesses were treated. For example, while the opposing witness was treated with "great respect," the court noted that both the accused student and his mother, an attorney, were told by panel members to "be quiet," with his mother being told to "shut up"; that a panel member had to be admonished to allow the accused student to speak; that a panel member made incorrect statements about the accused student's hospital records; and that the accused was "aggressively cross-examined" in general. Adding this disparate treatment to the fact that one of the panel members was Facebook friends with the key opposing witness and other procedural irregularities and flaws, the district court refused to dismiss the student's due process claims. After all, the court observed, "a fair and impartial tribunal and trial is a necessary component of procedural due process":

> The plaintiff's interest in avoiding expulsion is great, as is the benefit of an impartial panel in safeguarding against an erroneous decision. Nor does the providing of a fair and impartial tribunal impose a great administrative burden on the school. An impartial tribunal does not turn a university disciplinary hearing into an adversarial trial-type hearing.

In the criminal courts, a defendant may ask for a change in the location of a trial (a change of venue) when too much publicity or a heated atmosphere makes it virtually impossible to secure an impartial jury. In campus cases, an accused student all too often faces similar circumstances, but there is no means of changing the location. You face a steep uphill battle if you wish to contend that the general atmosphere on campus denied you an impartial hearing. Even if you show that there really was an emotionally charged and even poisonous atmosphere stacking the proverbial deck against you, you must prove that this atmosphere affected the hearing board's impartiality—a difficult burden to meet.

There have been many cases, however, where the

collective campus condemnation of an alleged offense makes it difficult for accused students to receive a fair hearing. One need only think of the rush to judgment by the campus community (and much of the nation) in the infamous 2006 case involving three members of the Duke University lacrosse team, who were accused of sexually assaulting a woman at a team party, to realize the grave risk of injustice presented by a public presumption of guilt. As Stuart Taylor and KC Johnson detail in their book, *Until Proven Innocent: Political Correctness and the Shameful Injustices of the Duke Lacrosse Rape Case*, the accused students faced hostility from, among many others, a group of 88 Duke faculty members who took out an advertisement condemning them and encouraging protests against them. In the end, the charges against the students were shown to be baseless.

Perhaps the best thing that you can do if you face a hearing in such hostile circumstances is to inform the board that you share the campus's general sentiment about the heinousness of the crime charged, and remind them of their duty to focus only on the facts of the specific case. Remind them that you are neither a symbol nor a scapegoat, but an individual who should be presumed to be innocent. Point out that there is *no* crime so heinous that innocence is an insufficient defense. And, of course, you should retain an attorney.

Although courts will sometimes overturn your campus conviction if you demonstrate actual bias, they do generally permit the presence of panelists who have a prior acquaintance with the matter at hand. In our civil and criminal systems of justice, judges must disqualify themselves if they have any prior substantial relationship with a matter before the court. However, courts recognize that in the intimate context of the university community, it is all but inevitable that fact-finders may have some prior acquaintance with the issues on which they are asked to pass judgment. Because few cases challenging the composition of university hearing boards are brought, it is not clear how much prior knowledge is too much. In *Nash v. Auburn University* (1987), the U.S. Court of Appeals for the Eleventh Circuit did not find a hearing board tainted by a panelist's knowing the suspicions against the defendant before serving on the panel. Indeed, the court found it permissible that the panelist had answered questions from some potential witnesses about how to come forward to offer testimony. Rulings in cases such as *Nash* imply, however, that if there *is* a level of more substantial previous involvement, as in *Marshall v. Maguire* and *Furey v. Temple University*, that would constitute a denial of impartiality. If you have evidence of a close prior relationship that harms the impartiality of the proceeding, you should certainly attempt to lodge a complaint.

In administrative agency proceedings generally, the individual making the decision to prosecute may not be significantly involved in determining guilt or innocence. In *Goss*, however, the Supreme Court refused to require separation of the judging and prosecutorial functions in minor high school disciplinary cases and even assumed that for short suspensions at high schools, the two roles would be performed by the same person.

In more serious cases, however, the prosecutor and judge very likely could *not* be the same person, because this would result in a decisionmaker with an unacceptable degree of bias and prior acquaintance with the matter. At the very least, you should argue that this is an unacceptable conflict if you are faced by such a situation.

Unfortunately, as of the publication of this *Guide*, risk management consultants, victims' rights advocates, and even the White House Task Force to Protect Students from Sexual Assault are strongly advocating for colleges and universities to adopt a so-called "single investigator" model for adjudicating campus claims of sexual harassment and sexual assault. This model proposes eliminating hearings altogether for students accused of assault and harassment and effectively empowering a sole administrator to serve as detective, judge, and jury. Troublingly, this system would afford the accused no meaningful chance to challenge his or her accuser's testimony. Nevertheless, the White House Task Force called the single investigator model "promising" and hailed its "very positive results" in a 2014 report. As defense attorneys (and FIRE Legal Network members) Matthew Kaiser and Justin Dillon wrote in a *Wall Street Journal* opinion piece in May 2014:

> [The White House Task Force] praises the so-called single-investigator model in which a

solitary "trained" investigator would handle the entire investigative and adjudicative process. In other words, one person—presumably paid by the university, whose federal funding may be at stake if the government says the institution has contravened Title IX—will effectively decide innocence or guilt. There is a name for a system like this, and it is Javert.

The Task Force evinced only the most meager sense of the rights necessary to secure fundamentally fair hearings, noting that it believes the single investigator model would still "safeguard[] an alleged perpetrator's right to notice and to be heard." FIRE remains deeply skeptical about this claim. At best, such a system would provide accused students with the *bare minimum* of due process required by the Constitution and any notion of fundamental fairness. At worst—and far more likely, given colleges' checkered track record with regard to respecting student due process rights—the single investigator system would allow a lone, self-interested administrator to find a student guilty of sexual assault without ever having to justify the finding to anyone but him or herself.

If the single investigator model is adopted by campuses nationwide—and, sadly, indications are that it may very well be—legal challenges to its constitutionality are all but inevitable. If you find yourself accused of sexual harassment or sexual assault and forced through a procedure in which you are not afforded a hearing or an opportunity to challenge the testimony of your accuser or his or her witnesses, be sure to check FIRE's website to learn more about what courts have said about the legality of such a system. You should also hire an attorney.

Hearing panels need not be of any minimum size, and there is no hard-and-fast rule about what percentage of the members of a panel is required in order to convict, although naturally it would have to be at least a majority. In serious cases where expulsion will result from a finding of guilt, FIRE strongly believes that whatever its composition, the hearing panel should reach a unanimous decision.

Training of the Hearing Panel and the Potential for Bias

Be aware that a hearing panel's impartiality is by no means a given. Indeed, it may be endangered by training that panel members are required by your college or university to attend as a condition of participation in the hearing process. For example, in 2011, FIRE released training materials used by Stanford University to train student jurors hearing sexual harassment and sexual assault cases that were aimed not at ensuring a fair trial for all parties, but rather at encouraging convictions of accused male students.

The training materials for Stanford's "Dean's Alternative Review Process" were largely derived from a book titled *Why Does He Do That: Inside the Minds of Angry and Controlling Men* and informed student participants that they should be "very, very cautious in accepting a man's claim that he has been wrongly accused of abuse or violence." The materials claimed that "[t]he great majority of allegations of abuse—though not all—are substantially accurate," and that "an abuser almost never 'seems like the type.'" Shockingly, the materials told jurors to believe that "act[ing] persuasive and logical" is a sign of guilt. Stanford also instructs campus tribunals that taking a neutral stand between the parties is the equivalent of siding with the accused.

Not all training will result in impermissible bias, of course. It is appropriate to train student and faculty panelists in the necessity of hearing both sides, considering all the evidence, understanding the standard of proof and the elements of the offense, and asking questions that might better reach the truth. Unfortunately, it is very easy to inject politicized or ideological viewpoints into panelist training, and it behooves you to ask pertinent questions about how panel members are prepared to undertake the serious task of determining responsibility for the charges levied against you.

Proof

BURDEN OF PROOF

The presumption of innocence—"innocent until proven guilty"—is central to our system of justice and our sense of fundamental fairness. When a public college seeks to discipline you, you should never have to prove your innocence. Rather, the college bears the burden of proving you guilty. Some evidence of your guilt, at least, has to be presented. You then must be given some opportunity to rebut the evidence.

STANDARD OF PROOF

The standard of proof that due process requires in university disciplinary proceedings—that is, the degree of certainty with which a fact must be established for the fact to be determined true—is a hotly debated topic. (Because of recent state and federal government mandates regarding the standard of proof in sexual harassment and sexual assault cases, this debate is particularly intense in that arena. See Part V for a fuller discussion of those mandates.) Because the presumption of innocence is one of the few due process protections afforded to college students, the standard of proof required to prove guilt is extremely important.

Colleges and universities do not have to employ the same standard of proof as the criminal justice system, where conviction has to rest on guilt that is certain "beyond a reasonable doubt." Nevertheless, some universities employ a greater standard of proof than the law requires—for example, the standard of "clear and convincing" evidence, which requires a reasonable certainty of guilt for conviction. At the *very least*, public colleges and universities must employ a "preponderance of evidence" standard, our judiciary's lowest standard, which requires that guilt be more likely than not for conviction. This is a *minimal* standard of proof necessary for conviction. After all, if the "preponderance" guideline is *not* met, this means that most of the evidence supports a finding of innocence rather than guilt. It would be a bizarre system that allowed convictions where innocence was more probable.

In theory, private university disciplinary panels must apply at least the "substantial evidence" standard of proof to disciplinary decisions. This protection flows from the legal doctrine that private university disciplinary decisions may not be "arbitrary and capricious" (see Part III). Courts have ruled that verdicts must be based on "substantial evidence" in order to avoid being arbitrary or capricious. If this doctrine were adhered to, the right to a decision based on "substantial evidence" would be one of the few procedural protections available to private university students. In practice, however, courts are reluctant to interfere with the disciplinary decisions of private universities, and they will do so only when such decisions are based on virtually no evidence.

DEFINITIONS: STANDARDS OF PROOF

The following different standards of proof are used by various college and university tribunals. They are defined here in the order of how difficult they are to meet, from the most to the least difficult.

Beyond a reasonable doubt: "fully satisfied, entirely convinced, satisfied to a moral certainty"

Clear and convincing evidence: "reasonable certainty of the truth ... the truth of the facts asserted is highly probable"

Preponderance of evidence: "more probable than not"

Substantial evidence: "such evidence that a reasonable mind might accept as adequate to support a conclusion"

Some evidence: any evidence at all supporting the charge

(Direct quotations are from *Black's Law Dictionary*.)

There are broad limits to the university's right to convict an individual on little or virtually no evidence, or on the basis of evidence that is overwhelmingly and very reliably contradicted. For example, if someone testified that you committed a crime on campus at a time when you have incontrovertible evidence that you were a thousand miles away, virtually any court would go out of its way to overturn your campus conviction. The victim's testimony that you were the culprit in that situation, although constituting "some" evidence, would not likely satisfy a court's notion of adequacy.

Procedure

FORMAL RULES OF EVIDENCE

What kind of evidence may and may not be used against a defendant in a college or university judicial proceeding? Due process does not require colleges and universities to apply the same rules governing the admissibility of evidence at criminal trials, although many universities do employ a few of those rules. In the criminal courts, witnesses may not testify (with some exceptions) to things that they don't know personally, but about which others have told them. That kind of testimony is called "hearsay," and it is generally barred from criminal proceedings. But because they are not bound by the standards of evidence applied in courts of law, university disciplinary tribunals may admit hearsay from witnesses as evidence—and most do. In the criminal courts, only sworn testimony is admissible from witnesses. In university tribunals, witnesses do not need to be put under oath. Indeed, at college or university trials, virtually anything may count as evidence. The only requirement is that the rules used allow for basic fairness. If the lack of formal rules of evidence denies you basic fairness, then you may have a due process claim.

CROSS-EXAMINATION

On similar grounds of rules essential to basic fairness, you may have the right to cross-examine the witnesses against you at a college or university disciplinary hearing, if such cross-examination is necessary to draw out the truth about the matter at issue. (Note, however, that recent government mandates imposed by the Department of Education's Office for Civil Rights have impacted the ability of students accused of sexual harassment and sexual assault to cross-examine witnesses, as explained in more detail in Part V.)

The Sixth Amendment guarantees the right to cross-examine witnesses in criminal proceedings. It also gives criminal defendants a right to confront their accusers—that is, to look at them eye to eye when they testify. The Sixth Amendment, however, even as extended by the Fourteenth Amendment, applies only to federal and state criminal proceedings. Whether a right to cross-examination would apply in public college disciplinary hearings depends upon whether it was essential to the "fair" hearing guaranteed by the due process clause.

A court may find cross-examination is required in cases hinging solely on factual claims and charges made orally by a witness. For example, in *Winnick v. Manning* (1972), the U.S. Court of Appeals for the Second Circuit noted that when a case involves "a problem of credibility," then allowing the accused to cross-examine witnesses might be "essential to a fair hearing." However, courts have generally been reluctant to find a due process violation on account of a denial of the right to cross-examine witnesses. Indeed, the Second Circuit found that Winnick, a University of Connecticut student suspended for participating in a campus demonstration, did not have a due process right to cross-examine witnesses at his hearing. Similarly, in *Gorman v. University of Rhode Island* (1988), the U.S. Court of Appeals for the First Circuit held that the student plaintiff did not have an "unlimited" right to cross-examine witnesses. The First Circuit opined: "The question presented is not whether the hearing was ideal, or whether its procedure could have been better. In all cases the inquiry is whether, under the particular circumstances presented, the hearing was fair, and accorded the individual the essential elements of due process." In other words, the fact that Gorman, the student, was not allowed to "cross-examine his accusers on his allegations of bias" wasn't enough to invalidate the fairness of the hearing.

The specific nature and scope of cross-examination required by due process depends on the circumstances. The logic of court decisions on this question is that limits on cross-examination that might be appropriate in one circumstance could be *inappropriate* in others, if it could be shown that such limits denied fundamental fairness to the accused. In *Donohue v. Baker* (1997), the U.S. District Court for the Northern District of New York found that it was permissible for the tribunal to allow the accused to question witnesses merely by posing his questions to the panel, which then directed them to the witness. Similarly, in *Gomes v. University of Maine System* (2005), the United States District Court for the District of Maine found that the University of Maine's placement of a

127

physical partition between the accuser and the accused during cross-examination that allowed the accused "a limited view" of the accuser did not violate the accused's right to due process. The court found that the partition "balance[ed] the need for the Complainant to be free of intimidation against the Plaintiffs' right to due process."

Even though the law requires cross-examination only in a limited set of circumstances, many schools allow for cross-examination at disciplinary hearings in a far greater range of situations. Once again, if your institution *promises* the right of cross-examination in a given situation, it may be legally obligated to live up to that promise.

Due process, as indicated by *Donohue* and *Gomes*, does not generally require face-to-face confrontation in campus disciplinary proceedings. However, if a compelling case could be made that such actual confrontation is necessary to a fair judgment (for example, when someone's defense is based on mistaken identity), it might be required by due process. As in the case with so many other protections, the extent of the "process that is due" depends largely upon the facts and circumstances of the situation. If you want to argue for more process, you need to demonstrate why such procedural rights are made necessary by the facts and circumstances of your particular case.

EXCULPATORY WITNESSES AND EVIDENCE

"Exculpatory" evidence is evidence that exculpates you of guilt—that is, that proves or serves to prove your innocence. It is the opposite of "inculpatory," or incriminating, evidence. In *Goss*, the Supreme Court did not require that students be permitted to call exculpatory witnesses in cases involving suspension of ten days or less. However, courts have long recognized that students have a right to call witnesses in cases where more serious punishment is at stake.

This principle, as applied to universities, originates from *Dixon v. Alabama State Board of Education* (1961), in which the United States Court of Appeals for the Fifth Circuit ordered that an accused student facing expulsion must be allowed to "produce either oral testimony or written affidavits of witnesses in his behalf." Although few courts have considered cases where this means of defending oneself was denied, in a serious case, due process would arguably be violated if the right to call exculpatory witnesses were not granted.

The right to call witnesses, however, does not appear to extend to a right to compel their attendance at the hearing. If you want the campus tribunal to make extra efforts to force or convince a reluctant witness to appear to testify, you should convince the panelists that the witness is essential to your defense. Again, this differs significantly from criminal trials, where you have a right to compel witnesses to testify in person if their testimony is at all relevant.

PRESUMPTIONS FROM SILENCE

Unlike a criminal court, a campus tribunal does not have to provide you the right to refuse to testify. Indeed, your silence at such a campus hearing *can* be used against you.

The Fifth Amendment guarantees that no person shall be compelled to incriminate himself in a criminal proceeding. It reflects a deep respect for the sanctity of a person's innermost being. As a result, accused persons may refuse to answer questions put to them in criminal proceedings—the celebrated "right to remain silent" announced in the *Miranda* warning. In criminal law, no inferences whatsoever, negative or positive, may be drawn from the silence of a criminal defendant.

While defendants have a right to remain silent in criminal court, students do *not* enjoy such a right at college disciplinary hearings, although a few universities do voluntarily provide this right. Your university may compel you to give testimony that may hurt you in any number of ways, and it may punish you or infer your guilt for refusing to testify.

However, if you make self-incriminating statements under compulsion in a public university disciplinary hearing—that is, if you are forced to make statements against your will because of severe penalties for silence—it is possible that these statements may not be used against you in criminal court. In *Garrity v. New Jersey* (1967), the Supreme Court of the United States established a general rule against the introduction, in criminal proceedings, of compelled statements from administrative hearings. This precedent has been applied to universities in cases such as *Furutani v. Ewigleben*, decided by the U.S. District Court for the Northern District of California in 1969.

More commonly, universities do not establish specific penalties for silence but state, instead, that a failure to testify will be weighed against the student. This is legally acceptable. The Supreme Court, in *Baxter v. Palmigiano* (1976), ruled that interpreting silence negatively is acceptable in administrative hearings if the use of the privilege not to testify is not directly punished. At least one court, the U.S. District Court for the District of New Hampshire, has applied this holding to university disciplinary hearings, in *Morale v. Grigel* (1976).

Unfortunately, testimony given under a threat that harmful inferences will be drawn from silence, rather than under a threat of direct penalties, is usually admissible in a criminal trial. In *Gabrilowitz v. Newman* (1978), the United States Court of Appeals for the First Circuit ruled that such testimony was voluntary, not compelled in any unconstitutional sense. The First Circuit noted that the University of Rhode Island disciplinary hearing at issue in *Gabrilowitz* did not involve compelled testimony, and the university rules "neither require[d] nor prohibit[ed] the drawing of an adverse inference from the silence of the accused." As a result, the accused student's testimony would be "entirely voluntary and subsequently admissible at the criminal case." The First Circuit conceded that the question of whether to testify in the college proceeding was tough, but just because the "choice facing [the student] is difficult, that does not make it unconstitutional."

In choosing whether to make a statement at your

disciplinary hearing, you should generally give the highest priority to protecting your interests in a potential criminal case, if one is pending, likely, or foreseeable. After all, the consequences of a criminal conviction are in almost all cases much graver than those imposed by a university. It is almost always a good strategy, therefore, to do everything possible to have your disciplinary hearing postponed until *after* the conclusion of your criminal case. If you are unable to secure a postponement, you should never assume that if you testify at the disciplinary proceeding, damaging statements will be inadmissible at a later criminal trial. Consult a lawyer fully familiar with the law in your jurisdiction if you need to know whether your campus testimony would be admissible in the criminal case. There is a common understanding among most attorneys and people of common sense: If you have something to hide, *for whatever reason,* it is almost always better to remain silent. Even if your university states that it will draw negative inferences from your silence, it is better to say nothing if what you say could potentially be incriminating in a criminal court.

It is all too easy to suffer from failing to follow this important and reasonable advice. For example, some students have been charged and convicted in criminal court on the basis of a mere apology given in the context of a campus proceeding. An accused student is sometimes told by a campus advisor that the tribunal might go easier on him if he apologizes—and this apology is later deemed evidence of guilt in criminal court. When the misconduct with which you are charged on campus is also a violation of the criminal law, proceed with the greatest caution, and secure the advice of an experienced, skilled criminal defense lawyer.

Open Versus Closed Proceedings

Criminal courts are open to the public in all but the most unusual circumstances. However, this is not the case in the university context because courts have held that unredacted student disciplinary records are "educational records" for purposes of the Family Educational Records Privacy Act, or FERPA. (For a more detailed discussion of FERPA, see Part IV, Section II.)

In deciding *Gonzaga University v. Doe* (2002), the Supreme Court treated disciplinary records as though they were effectively covered by FERPA. More to the point, in *United States v. Miami University* (2002), the U.S. Court of Appeals for the Sixth Circuit addressed the competing First Amendment and privacy interests raised by a student newspaper's attempt to obtain disciplinary records from a public university. The Sixth Circuit ultimately concluded that "student disciplinary records are education records," and thus protected by FERPA, "because they directly relate to a student and are kept by that student's university." The Sixth Circuit found that in contrast to criminal trials, "student disciplinary proceedings govern the relationship between a student and his or her university, not the relationship between a citizen and

'The People.'" As a result, "[o]nly the latter presumptively implicates a qualified First Amendment right of access to the proceedings and the records."

So at both public and private universities, your right to a closed hearing is guaranteed by FERPA. Colleges may not open a disciplinary hearing to the public unless the accused student consents to have it opened.

The only other individuals who sometimes have a right to attend disciplinary hearings are university staff members and, perhaps in certain cases, your parents. FERPA allows universities to share your educational records only with those staff members who have a "legitimate educational interest" in them. This means that you may prevent your university from opening your disciplinary hearing to individuals who have no legitimate purpose in being there. You will not be successful, however, if you object to the presence of staff members whose functions at the university relate to the matter.

As you might expect, administrators tend to opt for closed rather than open proceedings, because it is seen as easier to dispense campus justice (or injustice) outside of the public's critical gaze. You face a tough battle if you want your disciplinary hearing open to the public. At a private university you naturally have no right to an open hearing, because private universities can set virtually whatever rules they please, within reason. Courts have generally held that at public universities, due process does not require that a disciplinary hearing be open to the public, even if the student requests it. If, however, your college or university claims that it would like to grant your request but is prevented from doing so by FERPA, you may be able to prevail. FERPA gives the accused the right to a closed hearing; it does not prevent the accused from having an open one. You also may find it effective to make at least the moral argument that your hearing should be open to the public, asking your college or university what it has to hide.

Recordings and Transcripts of Proceedings

Having a record of the proceedings against you is extremely helpful, and you should seek to make a recording of any meetings or hearings you attend. The absence of a record makes both appeals and lawsuits against the university for wrongful actions far more difficult.

Courts have generally declined to hold that due process requires your college or university to make transcripts or recordings of the proceedings against you. However, in *Flaim v. Medical College of Ohio* (2005), the U.S. Court of Appeals for the Sixth Circuit voiced support for allowing students to make their own record. The court observed that "[w]hile due process may not impose upon the university the requirement to produce a record in all cases, fundamental fairness counsels that if the university will not provide some sort of record, it ought to permit the accused to record the proceedings if desired."

Moreover, if a university, public or private, has a rule requiring or permitting a recording or transcript, then that promise should be enforceable.

Nonetheless, many universities forbid the recording of disciplinary proceedings by anyone. If your university has a ban and you wish to create a record, you should challenge the rule as being without any reasonable basis or purpose. Remember that this allowance does not impose any cost on the university, so there is little justification for prohibiting it.

Complainants With a History of Lodging False Accusations

In the criminal justice system, the names of alleged crime victims typically become a matter of public record when a criminal case is brought. However, under educational records privacy laws (see Part IV: Section II), universities are obliged to keep confidential the names of persons who make accusations of misconduct. While the secrecy of the university disciplinary process has certain valuable aspects, it removes the great protection that the criminal justice system provides against false or malicious accusations. You have no way of knowing whether the person accusing you has made false accusations against other students on another or even many other occasions.

While the university itself is prohibited from informing you that your accuser has a history of lodging similar and demonstrably false accusations, the prior victims of this false accuser are not barred by law from speaking.

If you can find these individuals, they may be willing to testify on your behalf or otherwise help you. In a serious case, where you suspect you are being falsely accused by a person with a history of making false accusations, your lawyer may want to hire a professional investigator to examine whether this is the case. If you believe that publicity will not otherwise hurt your case, you may want to make your plight public in order to prompt others who have suffered at the hands of the same accuser to contact you. You might run into difficulty, however, if the university warns you to protect the privacy of your accuser and not to disclose his or her name. If your university has such a requirement, and you believe that it is hurting your case, you should make a detailed written presentation to the disciplinary tribunal explaining precisely why your defense will be hampered by your inability to conduct an investigation that uses the name of your accuser.

Similarly, if your accuser's name is secret, witnesses to whom the accuser may have made statements that could prove your innocence are less likely to come to light. Gathering evidence in a secret case is always more difficult than doing so in a well-publicized public proceeding.

SECTION IV: CONVICTION AND PUNISHMENT

Notice of Decision

Due process requires that you be informed promptly of the disciplinary board's decision in your case once it has been rendered.

In considering your case, the disciplinary panel does not need to reach a verdict. In the absence of evidence of your guilt, campus due process permits the panel to decide not to render any verdict at all, or to postpone the proceedings indefinitely until new evidence becomes available. This differs considerably from the criminal justice system, where, once accused, a defendant is entitled to a speedy trial and verdict.

Privacy laws bar universities from revealing the disposition of a disciplinary matter to complainants, except in the case of accusations involving violence or sex.

Written Findings

In recent years, courts have generally declined to find that due process requires written findings in student disciplinary cases. In *Flaim v. Medical College of Ohio*

(2005), the U.S. Court of Appeals for the Sixth Circuit held that "[a]n accused individual is generally not entitled to a statement of reasons for a decision against them, at least where the reasons for the decision are obvious." We know of no case where the lack of written rulings was seen as so outrageous an error that the disciplinary board's findings were overturned. This does not mean that no such case exists, but clearly this is not a common ground for judicially attacking a disciplinary outcome.

Many colleges and universities provide for written findings of fact or a written explanation of the reasoning behind the disciplinary panel's hearing, despite the state of the law. If your institution does not automatically provide written findings, it is a good idea to request them nonetheless. Written findings will be critical to your preparation of an appeal or legal challenge.

If your university has issued written findings in your case, and you believe that they contain lapses in logic, you may be able to use these findings in an internal appeal; or in a lawsuit alleging violation of due process, of the university's rules, or of state rules for administrative hearing boards. Courts have overruled disciplinary decisions on such grounds. In *Hardison v. Florida A&M University* (1998), for example, the Court of Appeal of Florida reversed a disciplinary panel's finding on the basis of the written findings. The university had convicted the student for assault and battery, but the court found that the facts reported in the written decision were insufficient to meet the applicable definition of assault and battery.

Appeal

The law does not require public universities to provide an appeal of student disciplinary decisions. Students have a constitutional right only to a single, reasonably fair internal hearing. However, the great majority of universities rightly allow an appeal. Reviewing a finding of guilt helps guarantee an accurate, reliable, and fair outcome.

Many institutions restrict the grounds for appeal to a certain limited subset of claims. Typically, these grounds require you to prove: (1) that the hearing or decision-making process was not carried out in conformity with prescribed policies and procedures, (2) that evidence unavailable at the time of the decision is now available (but note that evidence that was available but not submitted may be rejected), or (3) that the sanctions issued are disproportionate to the offense committed. Be sure to review your university's policies to ensure that your appeal complies with any requirements and limitations—it is better not to give administrators grounds to summarily reject your appeal.

Be aware, however, that an appeal sometimes can result in an *increase* in the severity of punishment. Before you decide to appeal an adverse verdict and punishment, check your college's handbook to see whether an appeal permits such an increase in penalties. If it does, then you should carefully weigh the risks and rewards of pursuing an appeal.

A meaningful appeal is an extremely important procedural protection, because it helps to ensure that all other procedural protections to which you are entitled actually were given to you. If the panel initially hearing your case knows that you have a right to appeal, it is more likely to treat your case properly, to avoid the embarrassment of its decision being reversed. When you argue for greater procedural protections at your initial hearing, you should make clear that you plan to appeal if you are not granted the safeguards that you believe you need for a fair trial.

Irregularities in the appeal process may be grounds for a contract claim against your university. For example, in the case of *Marshall v. Maguire* (1980), a New York state court overturned a college's decision against a student because of irregularities in the appeals process.

Even if your university *doesn't* have a formal appeal process, you should write to administrators to ask for reconsideration. You can write first to the supervisors of the disciplinary process or to the dean of students, and, if this fails, to the provost, president, and board of trustees. Always write as if these higher officials obviously would care about justice, fairness, and the truth of a case.

For a discussion of the accuser's right to appeal in sexual harassment or sexual assault hearings, as a result of recent administrative action by the Department of Education, see Part V.

Writing Letters of Complaint to University Officials

Many universities tell students involved in campus cases that because the disciplinary process is "confidential," defendants may not discuss their cases with anyone other than advisors, attorneys, or family members. Such policies have the effect, and too often the intention, of prohibiting students who are being mistreated from bringing their cases to the attention of the media and the university community. Nothing in federal law, including FERPA, prevents you from discussing your own case.

The administrators in charge of the disciplinary process would be hard pressed to accuse you of violating the university's confidentiality policy if you spoke about the abuses in disciplinary procedures with their superiors—namely the provost, the president, and even the trustees of your university. The duties of these officials include supervising the disciplinary process, so it is difficult to argue that it would be a breach of confidentiality to write to them. It is even probable that a public university student is entirely within his or her rights to bring unfair treatment to the attention of political figures such as legislators or the governor, on the theory that they are the ultimate heads of a public university system. (Recall that the First Amendment has a provision guaranteeing a citizen the right to "petition the government for a redress of grievances.")

If you find yourself facing abuses of power, you may want to write to one or more of these officials, all of whom might well be able to help your case. These officials may notice injustices that lower-level administrators ignore. The very act of complaining to a top university official might produce more meaningful review, because lower-level administrators will be in the unaccustomed position of having their superiors looking over their shoulders. Administrators often take pains to hide abuses from the attention of trustees. Complaining to trustees is a tactic that is too rarely used by aggrieved students. Sunlight, as Justice Louis Brandeis accurately said, is the best disinfectant.

Penalties

Universities enjoy wide discretion in determining the punishments chosen for particular infractions. Courts will typically defer to the judgments of university officials on matters of punishment, even if they think that the punishments are unwise, unfair, or excessive.

Nonetheless, a university may not impose a punishment that is drastically disproportionate to the offense for which the student has been found responsible. As the U.S. Court of Appeals for the Fifth Circuit put it in the high school case of *Lee v. Macon County Board of Education* (1974), "a school board could not constitutionally expel forever a pupil who had committed no offense other than being five minutes tardy one time." A punishment that is wildly out of proportion to the violation committed may cause a court to find a violation of substantive due process. Courts do not like to oversee a university's judicial system, but they often will react very negatively to unreasonable punitive extremes.

For example, in *Kickertz v. New York University* (2012),

the Appellate Division of the Supreme Court of New York vacated New York University's expulsion of a dental student who had been told fifteen minutes before she was to graduate that she had insufficient "credits" to do so. Specifically, NYU's dental program required students to perform $21,000 dollars worth of service to patients before graduating; Kickertz had performed $19,093. Other students had allegedly been allowed to make up shortfalls by performing treatments on family members, but Kickertz was denied this opportunity. Instead, Kickertz was allegedly instructed to simply make a payment for the difference directly to NYU, then fill out false paperwork to make it appear as though she had completed her requirement. After following this alleged instruction, Kickertz—who, in the meantime, had finished her revenue-generating obligations, ultimately earning over $23,000 for NYU—was found guilty by NYU's ethics board of falsifying records. She was expelled a few months later without notice or a hearing and denied both her graduate and undergraduate degrees, as she'd been enrolled in a joint program.

Kickertz filed suit. On review, the Appellate Division held that "NYU did not substantially comply with its own published guidelines and policies," also finding that Kickertz "was not given a fair opportunity to cross-examine her accusers, and key procedural rulings were made and/or influenced by" self-interested NYU officials. The court also noted the disproportionate punishment for Kickertz's alleged error and the fact that other students had been treated differently in the same situation. All told, the court concluded that Kickertz's treatment "shocks one's sense of fairness" and vacated her expulsion.

Student defendants often ask whether public universities may punish them by removing them from extracurricular activities such as sports or by suspending them from aspects of campus life such as on-campus housing. These sanctions are permissible. Universities may also punish students by asking them to attend courses or workshops designed to help them avoid misconduct, such as meetings for alcohol or substance abuse or anger management classes. It is probably unlawful, however, for public universities to *force* you to attend programs the goal of which is your adoption of officially sanctioned views on controversial topics such as race, sex, or sexual orientation, even if your offenses relate to your views on these subjects. (See FIRE's *Guide to First-Year Orientation and Thought Reform on Campus* for more on this topic.)

Fines are also acceptable as punishments, as long as they are not so excessive as to put a grossly unequal burden on rich and poor students. In the latter case, a campus appeal might successfully be pursued on grounds of economic discrimination and disparate treatment on the basis of economic status. Such grounds might not succeed in court, but they might have substantial moral force in a campus appeal.

Reporting of Crimes to Police and Prosecutors

If you are found responsible for a crime of violence or a sex offense, your university may choose to report your name and the fact of the finding of responsibility to the police and to the local district attorney. Without a sub-poena—that is, without a formal, written and (usually) court-authorized order, the university may disclose only your name, the accusation, and the final result.

Be advised that it is easy for police, grand juries, or, in some jurisdictions, victims' attorneys seeking monetary damages in civil suits to obtain a subpoena for all of the university's records related to your case. The university is required to make a reasonable effort to inform you that it received a subpoena for your records before comply-ing with it, unless the subpoena requires the university not to give such notice. Individuals can be subpoenaed, as well. If university officials are subpoenaed and asked questions about your records, they must answer. Addi-tionally, if the campus police created its own file on you independently of the university administration, they may freely share these records with prosecutors.

When very serious crimes have been reported to the local police or campus security, the university has a re-sponsibility to warn the campus community that such crimes have occurred under the Clery Act of 1990.

If you learn of prosecutorial interest in your con-duct, you should consult a criminal defense attorney immediately.

PART V: SEXUAL HARASSMENT AND SEXUAL ASSAULT

Since the publication of the first edition of this *Guide*, the most dangerous threats to students' due process rights have been posed by largely well-intentioned but misguided efforts to address sexual harassment and sexual assault on campus. Legislative and regulatory requirements introduced in recent years at the state and federal levels have substantially altered the way in which both public and private institutions must respond to allegations of sexual harassment and sexual assault. Common-sense and previously commonplace protections—like the right to question one's accuser, or to be innocent until found guilty by clear and convincing evidence—have been prohibited in an effort to make campus judicial systems more "equitable." Under substantial pressure from federal regulators, politicians, student and alumni activists, and the local and national media, campuses nationwide have abandoned due process protections for students accused of sex-related offenses, sharply reducing

149

the likelihood of a just outcome or a fair hearing.

The national debate about precisely how much process is due to college students accused of sexual assault rages on as of this *Guide*'s publication. By the time you read this, new laws may have been passed and new regulations may have been enacted, further impacting the due process rights you possess and the means available to you to clear your name. Nevertheless, this updated *Guide* would be grossly incomplete if it did not explain the relevant issues and legal concepts that govern sexual harassment and sexual assault adjudication on campus. While you should keep in mind that the situation remains very much in flux, we aim here to provide you with a useful survey of the landscape to help you prepare your defense against these very serious charges. Note that our review here is not simply descriptive, but critical, as well; we strongly believe that many of the regulations and statutes described below present a threat to due process protections and fundamental fairness. After reading this section, we strongly recommend visiting FIRE's website, thefire.org, to ensure you have access to the latest information regarding your rights when accused of sexual harassment and sexual assault.

Why Do Colleges Adjudicate Sexual Harassment and Sexual Assault?

When the subject of campus sexual harassment and assault is broached, one question is almost always asked:

Why are colleges handling sexual assault, anyway? Isn't that a job for the police? After all, colleges don't adjudicate murder, perhaps the only crime more heinous than rape. So why is sexual assault different?

These are excellent questions. Because of the seriousness of the alleged offense, a reasonable observer might be surprised that colleges and universities prosecute sexual assault claims internally, independently of law enforcement. College tribunals are well suited for plagiarism charges, as those allegations concern academic work and thus the special expertise of academic administrators might usefully be brought to bear. They might also adjudicate relatively minor cases against property, such as stealing dinnerware from the campus cafeteria. But fairly determining whether an accused student is guilty of sexual assault requires skills beyond the university's competence—the ability to gather and analyze forensic evidence, for example. So it may not be immediately clear why institutions of higher education are involved with such serious charges at all.

The answer is that colleges and universities that receive federal funding—the vast majority of institutions, both public and private—are required by federal anti-discrimination law to respond to allegations of sexual harassment and sexual assault.

Title IX of the Education Amendments of 1972 prohibits discrimination based on sex in educational programs or activities operated by recipients of federal funding. Sexual harassment has been recognized as a form of sex discrimination under Title IX by federal courts for decades. As a result, colleges and universities receiving federal funding—again, that's virtually all of them—must maintain policies addressing sexual harassment.

Likewise, both federal courts and the Department of Education's Office for Civil Rights (OCR), the federal agency responsible for enforcing Title IX, have found that sexual assault is a particularly egregious form of sexual harassment. For example, in *Soper v. Hoben* (1999), the United States Court of Appeals for the Sixth Circuit found that rape "obviously qualifies as being severe, pervasive, and objectively offensive sexual harassment." Other courts have reached the same conclusion, and OCR has stated that "a single instance of rape is sufficiently severe to create a hostile environment." (Harassment that creates a "hostile environment" is prohibited by Title IX, per OCR regulations.) Under this framework, colleges must adjudicate sexual assault, too, despite a lack of expertise or competency to do so.

So the simple answer is that colleges and universities handle sexual harassment and sexual assault claims because federal law requires them to do so. This is not necessarily the only reason, however. Even without being compelled to do so as a condition of receiving federal funding, some institutions might adjudicate these claims in an effort to stem legal liability, as a matter of institutional autonomy, or because their students expect them to. But Title IX makes their involvement mandatory.

What Does Title IX Require?

Under Title IX, colleges and universities that know or should have known about sexual harassment that creates a hostile environment—including sexual assault, as explained above—are required to take immediate action to eliminate the harassment, prevent it from reoccurring, and respond to its effects. That's the basic rule set forth by OCR. Of course, the details are of crucial importance: What kind of conduct qualifies as sexual harassment that creates a hostile environment? What kind of immediate action must the school take? How can an institution fulfill its obligation to prevent the harassment from happening again, and how might it address the harassment's effects? All of these questions—and their impact on due process rights—are discussed in greater detail below.

But first, when examining Title IX's requirements, it is important to consider the language of the law itself separately from the law's implementing regulations.

The central text of Title IX itself is brief and to the point: "No person in the United States shall, on the basis of sex, be excluded from participation in, be denied the benefits of, or be subjected to discrimination under any education program or activity receiving Federal financial assistance." The statute then lists a series of exempted organizations and activities, including the merchant marines, certain religious institutions, and fraternities and sororities. That's essentially it.

In contrast, Title IX's implementing regulations provide far more detailed, specific requirements for colleges and universities. (Implementing regulations are the rules promulgated by an enforcement agency to ensure statutory compliance.) OCR has enacted regulations and issued guidance documents over the years in an attempt to ensure that Title IX's broad ban on sex discrimination is enforced effectively on campus. Indeed, OCR's most recent guidance, announced in 2011 and described in further detail below, are so voluminous, controversial, and confusing that the agency was forced to issue a separate, 46-page-long "Frequently Asked Questions" document to clarify the regulations to frustrated administrators. After all, campuses that fail to comply with OCR's interpretation of Title IX's requirements risk an embarrassing investigation by the agency and the possibility of losing their federal funding. So no matter how confusing or seemingly far-removed from the statute's core text, OCR's interpretation of Title IX is *de facto* law on today's campuses.

While OCR's view of Title IX's requirements is effectively binding, it is important to recognize that OCR is an agency within the executive branch. This structural fact constrains the agency's power in two ways. First, OCR's leadership is likely to change with the arrival of each new President, who is empowered to appoint his or her own Secretary of Education (to lead the Department of Education) and Assistant Secretary for Civil Rights (to lead the Office for Civil Rights). As OCR's leadership shifts, so too might its understanding of Title IX. Further, were OCR's interpretation of Title IX or the other federal anti-discrimination laws it enforces to become politically untenable, the President or the electorate could force a shift in leadership or policy.

Second, because of the formidable power invested in federal agencies like OCR to interpret federal law, Congress passed the Administrative Procedure Act of 1946 (APA). Designed to protect democratic decisionmaking from being undermined by administrative fiat, the APA requires agencies to adhere to formal procedures before enacting regulations that affect citizens. These procedures include staging a "notice-and-comment" period before agency rulemaking, wherein the agency informs the public of its proposed regulations, the public responds, and the agency explains how its final regulations respond to public concerns. Through this and other requirements, the APA provides a degree of accountability and transparency to the actions of federal agencies like OCR.

Sexual Assault and Due Process

The Department of Education's Office for Civil Rights has enforced institutional compliance with Title IX for decades. But beginning in 2011, the agency became far more aggressive and prescriptive in regulating university responses to allegations of sexual assault. Following the Office for Civil Rights' lead, federal and state legislators began debating and passing legislation governing sexual assault on campus shortly thereafter. As a result of these changes—and more seem likely to follow—colleges and universities are required to treat sexual assault claims differently from other alleged violations of university policy. Unfortunately, the administrative and legislative activity thus far has been almost uniformly dismissive of the due process rights of the accused, stripping procedural protections and making just results less likely. In order to understand what rights you do and do not possess in sexual harassment or sexual assault hearings, it is important to review each of these changes and their origin.

2011 "Dear Colleague" Letter

In April 2011, the Office for Civil Rights issued a policy statement on the subject of "sexual violence" to college and university administrators nationwide. Taking the form of a "Dear Colleague" letter—its opening salutation greets recipients as "Dear Colleague"—the statement from then-Assistant Secretary for Civil Rights Russlynn Ali announced OCR's new understanding of how colleges must respond to allegations of sexual harassment and sexual assault in order to comply with Title IX. Despite the fact that the new mandates prescribed by the Dear Colleague letter were either unprecedented or broke with previous OCR guidance, the agency did not subject the letter's requirements to public notice-and-comment, as required by the Administrative Procedure Act. As detailed below, OCR's new requirements erode due process for accused students in serious and substantive ways.

STANDARD OF EVIDENCE

OCR's 2011 "Dear Colleague" letter mandated that colleges and universities receiving federal assistance employ a "preponderance of the evidence" standard within their grievance procedures governing sexual harassment and sexual assault. Per OCR's letter, under Title IX, the "prompt and equitable resolution" of allegations concerning sexual harassment and sexual violence requires application of the "preponderance of the evidence standard (*i.e.*, it is more likely than not that sexual harassment or violence occurred)."

OCR's interpretation of Title IX to require the use of the preponderance of the evidence standard broke new ground; this requirement had not previously been "discovered" in the law. In fact, OCR had previously granted universities far greater flexibility with regard to both the standard of proof used and other procedural details. For example, OCR's 2001 *Revised Sexual Harassment Guidance*, which governed Title IX compliance until the 2011 letter, explicitly recognized that "procedures adopted by schools will vary considerably in detail, specificity, and components, reflecting differences in audiences, school sizes and administrative structures, state or local legal requirements, and past experience." The 2011 "Dear Colleague" letter revoked this discretion—and with it, institutions' ability to grant students due process protections that are appropriate for the gravity of the offenses of which they are accused.

The preponderance of the evidence standard is our

judiciary's lowest evidentiary threshold that still allows for the presumption of innocence, and the "Dear Colleague" letter explicitly ruled out the use of higher standards of proof in sexual misconduct cases. OCR argued that university judicial systems using the "clear and convincing" standard—which requires proof that "it is highly probable or reasonably certain that the sexual harassment or violence occurred"—are "not equitable" and therefore violate Title IX. (Of course, both the preponderance of the evidence standard and the clear and convincing evidence standard fall far short of the "beyond a reasonable doubt" standard required in criminal cases.)

OCR's mandate is in tension with Supreme Court rulings like *Goss v. Lopez* (1975) and *Addington v. Texas* (1979). In *Goss*, as discussed earlier in this *Guide*, the Court held that when "a person's good name, reputation, honor, or integrity is at stake because of what the government is doing to him," due process requires "precautions against unfair or mistaken findings of misconduct and arbitrary exclusion from school." The Court made these observations about due process protections at the elementary and secondary school level, finding at least minimal requirements of due process necessary because disciplinary action "could seriously damage the students' standing with their fellow pupils and their teachers as well as interfere with later opportunities for higher education and employment." Given the increased likelihood of much further-reaching negative consequences for a college student found guilty of sexual harassment or sexual violence in a campus judicial proceeding, greater protections are required, not lesser.

And in *Addington,* the Court—"mindful that the function of legal process is to minimize the risk of erroneous decisions"—noted that an intermediate standard of proof (*i.e.,* the clear and convincing standard) might properly be used "in civil cases involving allegations of fraud or some other quasi-criminal wrongdoing by the defendant." The Court arrived at this conclusion because the "interests at stake in those cases are deemed to be more substantial than mere loss of money," and using the clear and convincing standard "reduce[s] the risk to the defendant of having his reputation tarnished erroneously by increasing the plaintiff's burden of proof." As FIRE pointed out in a May 2011 response to OCR's "Dear Colleague" letter, college sexual assault hearings involve allegations of felony criminal conduct, and the interests implicated certainly go beyond the mere loss of money.

In the 2011 "Dear Colleague" letter, OCR argued that the preponderance of the evidence standard is appropriate for adjudicating sexual assault and sexual harassment claims because it is the same standard that federal courts use when deciding civil lawsuits, including civil rights lawsuits. But as FIRE and others have noted, the use of this low burden of proof in federal civil cases is counterbalanced by the many procedural safeguards provided to defendants in those cases—safeguards that aren't present in campus cases. To provide just a few examples:

- Defendants in civil trials have their hearings conducted by experienced and impartial judges.
- Either party can ask a jury to determine findings of fact.
- Either party may be represented by an attorney.
- The rules of "discovery" allow each party to gather necessary evidence from the other side upon request.
- Hearsay and other forms of unreliable evidence are typically excluded from the proceeding, and all testimony is given under sworn oath.

None of these protections are guaranteed in campus sexual assault hearings, rendering the comparison between the use of the preponderance of the evidence standard in civil court and campus hearings wholly inappropriate. And while defendants in civil lawsuits have the option to settle out of court and keep the matter private, students found guilty by campus tribunals have no such option, virtually guaranteeing that a negative outcome will have a lifelong effect.

The evidentiary standard may fairly be described as an accused student's most significant procedural protection. By lowering it for those accused of sexual harassment and sexual assault, OCR has confused an increased number of convictions with increased justice.

RIGHT TO AN APPEAL

OCR's "Dear Colleague" letter dictates that institutions

must provide the accuser a right to appeal if the accused is provided that right. This allowance—now codified in federal law under the Violence Against Women Act Reauthorization, discussed in more detail below—permits an accuser to appeal the outcome of a campus hearing that has cleared the accused of wrongdoing, requiring the accused to defend him- or herself repeatedly. Forcing students who have been found not guilty of sexual harassment or sexual assault to submit to yet another hearing undermines due process for several reasons. After all, there's a reason that the prosecution isn't allowed to appeal acquittals in the criminal justice system.

First, students who have proven the charges against them to be baseless may now effectively be tried all over again, at a great cost of time, energy, and money. Dragging students already found not guilty through the process again is neither "prompt" nor "equitable," contrary to OCR's requirements for grievance procedures under Title IX. In fact, it resembles a violation of a criminal law defense called "double jeopardy," whereby someone accused of a crime cannot be tried for the same charges again once the original hearing has properly ended in either acquittal or conviction. For the same reasons of fundamental fairness that our criminal justice system does not allow those accused of crimes to face double jeopardy, colleges and universities should not force their students to face a second hearing for the same charge.

Second, pursuant to OCR's "Dear Colleague" letter, accused students are already subjected to an inappropriately low standard of proof. Allowing accusers to appeal a finding of innocence only amplifies the due process problems introduced by OCR's "preponderance of the evidence" mandate.

Finally, given the publicity and emotion that often surround complaints of sexual harassment and sexual assault, the panel or administrator hearing the appeal may often be under significant pressure to return a "correct" verdict: guilty. Accordingly, it's far from certain that accused students who have already been cleared once will be able to receive the impartial hearing they deserve. What's more, each college and university has its own appeals process, and the resulting variability makes a blanket rule regarding dual appeals more dangerous. For example, some campuses put a single person in charge of hearing appeals. In these situations, the risk of injustice sharply increases, as that person may be empowered to rehear the case with no procedural oversight.

CROSS-EXAMINATION

While not banning cross-examination outright, OCR's "Dear Colleague" letter takes a clear stand against its allowance in sexual harassment and sexual assault proceedings on campus. The letter states that "OCR strongly discourages schools from allowing the parties personally to question or cross-examine each other during the hearing," contending that "[a]llowing an alleged perpetrator to question an alleged victim directly may be traumatic or intimidating, thereby possibly escalating or perpetuating a hostile environment."

OCR's across-the-board disapproval ignores the importance of cross-examination, declared by the Supreme Court in *California v. Green* (1970) to be the "greatest legal engine ever invented for the discovery of truth." Although the Court has not found cross-examination to be a general procedural requirement for college discipline cases, as discussed above, lower courts have recognized it as necessary in certain instances. For example, in *Winnick v. Manning* (1972), the United States Court of Appeals for the Second Circuit held that cross-examination in campus proceedings may be "essential to a fair hearing" in cases that involve "a problem of credibility." Given the prevalence of so-called "he-said, she-said" scenarios in sexual assault cases, which are often marked by drug and alcohol use and a lack of witnesses, the credibility of all parties is routinely at issue.

Other courts have reached similar conclusions. For example, because students have a right to a fundamentally fair procedure, the United States Court of Appeals for the Eleventh Circuit found in *Nash v. Auburn University* (1987) that "[d]ue process requires that appellants have the right to respond" to accusing witnesses and to ask those witnesses questions through the official presiding over the hearing. In *Furey v. Temple University* (2012), the United States District Court for the Eastern District of Pennsylvania held that "due process require[s] that the plaintiff be able to cross-examine witnesses" in cases where an accuser's testimony might be determinative, serving as "an important safeguard" because the "purpose of cross-examination is to ensure that issues of credibility and truthfulness are made clear to the decision makers." Likewise, in *Donohue v. Baker* (1997), the United States District Court for the Northern District of New York noted the particular importance of cross-examination in campus sexual assault hearings, finding that "due process required" that a student accused of sexual assault be allowed to "direct questions to his accuser."

To the extent that OCR allows cross-examination if the accused's questions are funneled through a third party, as considered in *Donohue*, it is important that the third party—be it an administrator or the hearing panel—not be allowed to reject certain questions out of hand without clearly stated and objectively reasonable grounds for doing so. The exclusion of any given line of questioning must be previously known to both parties and the panel before the proceeding begins, and it must be limited only to those matters that are entirely and obviously unrelated to determining the veracity of the charge leveled against the accused.

EQUAL TREATMENT FOR BOTH PARTIES

While overwhelmingly damaging to student due process rights, the "Dear Colleague" letter does nevertheless provide some useful clarity regarding certain aspects of the hearing process OCR expects recipient institutions to administer. For example, the letter emphasizes the necessity of equal treatment for both the complainant and the accused student with regard to many aspects of the hearing process, including but not limited to access to information to be used in the hearing, access to counsel and participation of counsel, the ability to review the other party's statements, access to pre-hearing meetings, and equal opportunities to present witnesses and evidence. If one party is granted these allowances, OCR indicates that the other must be, as well. Additionally, OCR recommends that recipient institutions provide accused students with a procedure for appeal and instructs recipient institutions to "maintain documentation of all proceedings, which may include written findings of facts, transcripts, or audio recordings." These recommendations will help ensure that decisions unsupported by available evidence will not stand. These mandates are helpful, and students accused of sexual misconduct should not be shy about demanding their institution's adherence to them.

RESPONSE TO THE "DEAR COLLEAGUE" LETTER

Colleges have almost universally adopted the changes mandated by the April 2011 "Dear Colleague" letter, including the primary requirements described above. Unsurprisingly, this sea change in how colleges respond to sexual assault has proven intensely controversial.

Advocacy groups have weighed in on both sides of the

issue. Student activist groups like Know Your IX have captured national attention by highlighting the shocking stories of students whose sexual assault allegations were ignored or mishandled by inept or dismissive administrators. Marshaling support across campuses, these victims' rights groups have successfully lobbied for legislative action at both the state and federal levels, as discussed below. Meanwhile, while acknowledging the need to more effectively combat sexual assault on campus, both civil liberties groups like FIRE and professional organizations like the American Association of University Professors have repeatedly criticized OCR's disregard for due process protections. College administrators and attorneys have also criticized OCR's new mandates, as institutions that fail to alter their procedures for handling sexual harassment and sexual assault allegations risk formal federal investigation by OCR and the loss of federal funding.

Nevertheless, colleges nationwide have been virtually uniform in their adoption of OCR's new requirements. Perhaps unsurprisingly, a legion of private consultant groups has blossomed in the wake of the new mandates, as attorneys charge handsome sums to assist with Title IX compliance. Indeed, several former OCR staff attorneys left government work following the "Dear Colleague" letter to work at institutions like Harvard University as Title IX Coordinators, an administrative position imbued with greatly expanded powers and responsibilities under the new requirements.

ENFORCEMENT

Since issuing the 2011 "Dear Colleague" letter, OCR has redoubled its emphasis on enforcement. Following prompting from the White House Task Force to Protect Students from Sexual Assault, a body commissioned in 2014 and chaired by Vice President Joe Biden, OCR released for the first time a list of all colleges and universities under investigation by the agency for "possible violations of federal law over the handling of sexual violence and harassment complaints." As of press time, this list has grown to include over 85 separate cases at 85 institutions—an increase of 50 percent compared to the number of investigations disclosed to the public just six months prior.

To date, OCR has rarely if ever used the enforcement mechanisms available to it. The agency has not eliminated any institution's federal funding, and has very seldom instructed the Department of Justice to initiate litigation against an institution. Instead, most colleges and universities facing investigation eventually enter into a "resolution agreement" with OCR, promising to undertake a number of remedial actions, which often include altering institutional policies, creating significant new administrative duties, and conducting "climate surveys" on campus. But the mere threat of an investigation has proven to be a powerful motivator, and the vast majority of institutions facing an investigation comply with OCR's demands.

OCR investigations typically concern allegations of an institution's failure to properly respond to the alleged victim's claims or to maintain policies that comply with OCR's mandates under the 2011 "Dear Colleague" letter. Interestingly, however, OCR initiated an investigation at Brandeis University in the fall of 2014 that concerns whether an accused student was afforded a fair hearing by the university. This may be the first time that OCR has investigated a school for an alleged failure to properly ensure fundamental fairness to the accused.

If you believe your college or university has failed to meet its obligation to handle the allegations of sexual harassment or sexual assault levied against you in a fair way, it is important to file a complaint with the Office for Civil Rights and to let your institution know you have done so. Your college or university is legally barred from retaliating against you for bringing your concerns to OCR's attention.

LITIGATION

The erosion of due process rights required by the "Dear Colleague" letter has also prompted widespread litigation. Accused students have responded to expulsions and suspensions by filing a wave of lawsuits against their institutions after being found guilty of sexual assault in proceedings that they claim lack basic fairness. As of press time, nearly 30 students have filed such suits, alleging a range of claims including the violation of constitutional due process rights and breach of contract due to failure to adhere to published procedures. Some lawsuits have even alleged the violation of Title IX itself, claiming that the denial of due process protections mandated by the "Dear Colleague" letter so dramatically tilts the scales against male students as to render them guilty as a function of their gender. This is a high hurdle for plaintiffs to clear, and it bears watching to see if any plaintiffs have success on such a claim.

As this *Guide* was heading to publication, some courts had shown a willingness to entertain the claims of accused students, indicating an agreement that the processes employed by defendant colleges may have failed to provide the plaintiffs with fundamentally fair procedures. For example, in *King v. DePauw University* (2014), the United States District Court for the Southern District of Indiana issued a preliminary injunction preventing DePauw University from suspending a male student found guilty of sexual assault. After reviewing DePauw's handling of the allegations against the student, the court found that the student's Title IX claim was unlikely to succeed, finding insufficient evidence that "DePauw has, or would, treat a female student accused of sexual misconduct less favorably than it has treated its male students in that position." But the court granted the injunction based on the student's breach of contract claim, identifying a number of problems in DePauw's handling of the case: the fact that the investigation of the incident proceeded only after a "substantial" delay; DePauw's refusal to grant the student additional time to prepare for his hearing; the hearing panel's almost exclusive reliance on witnesses provided by the accusing student; the "incomplete nature" of the panel's questions at the hearing; and the fact that the accusing student's advisor is married to DePauw's Title IX Coordinator, who played a key role in obtaining statements heard by the panel.

Given these concerns, and concluding that the student would suffer "irreparable harm" were the suspension imposed while the case went to trial, the court issued an injunction prohibiting DePauw from suspending the student. Interestingly, in analyzing the harm that would be visited upon the student were the injunction not granted, the court identified the high stakes for a student accused of sexual assault:

> The Court also finds that King has demonstrated that he will suffer irreparable harm if an injunction is not entered. If King is not permitted to complete this upcoming semester at DePauw—even if, as DePauw asserts, he could choose to attend another university and ultimately graduate on time—he will forever have either a gap or a senior-year transfer on his record. The Court finds it inevitable that he would be asked to explain either situation by future employers or graduate school admissions committees, which would require him to reveal that he was found guilty of sexual misconduct by DePauw. Successfully seeing this lawsuit to its conclusion could not erase the gap or the transfer; the question will still be

raised, and any explanation is unlikely to fully erase the stigma associated with such a finding. Money damages would not provide an adequate remedy at that point; DePauw's disciplinary finding—even if determined to have been arbitrary or made in bad faith—would continue to affect him in a very concrete way, likely for years to come.

The court's awareness of the life-altering impact of a guilty finding is noteworthy, especially given the absence of such awareness on the part of the Department of Education's Office for Civil Rights and administrators nationwide. As FIRE has argued, the serious harms identified by the court in *King* make a case for greater due process protections, not lesser. As cases like *King* progress through the courts, they may well alter the current legal landscape for students accused of such serious misconduct. A judicial rebuke of OCR's administrative demands could yet vindicate student due process rights.

Legislation

OCR's mandates do not represent the only changes to how colleges and universities address allegations of sexual assault that are required by the government. In addition to OCR's administrative requirements, both state and federal lawmakers have passed legislation that impacts the rights afforded to students accused of sexual assault.

VIOLENCE AGAINST WOMEN ACT REAUTHORIZATION: CAMPUS SAVE ACT

In March 2013, President Barack Obama signed the Violence Against Women Reauthorization Act (VAWA) into law. FIRE takes no position on the vast majority of the law, as most of it does not concern student rights. However, VAWA as passed did contain elements of a bill originally known as the Campus Sexual Violence Elimination Act (the "Campus SaVE Act") that concern collegiate responses to allegations of sexual assault. These requirements, now passed into federal law, are worth reviewing.

First, VAWA requires colleges and universities to publicly disclose the standard of evidence they employ in sexual assault hearings. (Previous drafts of VAWA required use of the "preponderance of the evidence" standard. After lobbying from FIRE and others, that requirement was removed before VAWA was passed into law.) VAWA requires that your college or university publish the range of sanctions and remedial measures possible following a finding of sexual assault, as well as a statement on how the institution will protect the privacy of the victim. VAWA also requires that both parties in a sexual assault hearing be provided written notice, at the same time, of the results of the proceeding and the appeal procedures, as well as any updates to the result as it progresses through the process. With respect to appeals, VAWA also codified the "Dear Colleague" letter's requirement that if the opportunity to appeal is provided to one party, it must also be provided to the other.

Perhaps most importantly, VAWA states that "the accuser and the accused are entitled to the same opportunities to have others present during an institutional disciplinary proceeding, including the opportunity to be accompanied to any related meeting or proceeding by an advisor of their choice." This means that students accused of sexual assault may have an advisor—including an attorney—with them as the case against them proceeds. This is a very valuable protection, and if accused of such serious misconduct, you should take advantage of it. You are far more likely to secure a just result with the participation of an attorney or a competent advisor.

The Department of Education has issued regulations interpreting this VAWA provision to allow schools to promulgate "restrictions regarding the extent to which the advisor may participate in the proceedings, as long as the restrictions apply equally to both parties." FIRE opposes this interpretation. The statute is silent as to whether an institution may limit the advisor's participation, and reading into it a right to restrict advisor participation has the unfortunate potential to eliminate the usefulness of an advisor altogether. Silencing an advisor dramatically reduces his or her potential ability to help and conflicts with some state laws, like North Carolina's "right to counsel" law, described earlier. Regardless of this regulation, you should demand that your advisor be able to participate as fully as necessary to secure justice.

"AFFIRMATIVE CONSENT"

In the fall of 2014, California Governor Jerry Brown signed Senate Bill 967 (SB 967) into law, requiring all state universities and private universities that receive state funding to adopt an "affirmative consent" policy. (SB 967 also codifies the use of the "preponderance of the evidence" standard in sexual assault cases on campus, eroding a crucial due process protection for students accused of serious criminal conduct, as discussed above.) This confusing and legally unworkable standard now governs consent to sexual activity on virtually every California campus. Shortly after SB 967 became law, New York Governor Andrew Cuomo ordered all 64 State University of New York campuses to adopt a similar policy. Other states and university systems are considering similar policy changes as of press time.

Generally speaking, affirmative consent posits that sexual activity is sexual assault unless the non-initiating party's consent is, as SB 967 puts it, an "affirmative, conscious, and voluntary agreement to engage in sexual activity" that is "ongoing throughout a sexual activity." In SB 967's formulation, consent "can be revoked at any time," and it is the "responsibility of each person involved in the sexual activity to ensure that he or she has the affirmative consent of the other or others to engage in the sexual activity." The bill forbids the accused from pleading confusion over consent as a defense if he or she "did not take reasonable steps, in the circumstances known to the accused at the time, to ascertain whether the complainant affirmatively consented."

In contrast, the SUNY definition does not explicitly require "ongoing" consent. But by positing that "[c]onsent to any one form of sexual activity cannot automatically imply consent to any other forms of sexual activity," the SUNY policy seemingly has the same practical impact. Of course, the boundaries separating "one form of sexual activity" and "any other forms of sexual activity" are all but certain to prove subjective and unclear.

There is no practical, fair, or consistent way for colleges (or, for that matter, courts) to ensure that "affirmative consent" rules for sexual intercourse are followed. It is impracticable for the government to require students to obtain affirmative consent at each stage of a physical encounter and to later prove that attainment in a campus hearing. Under affirmative consent regimes, a student could be found guilty of sexual assault and deemed a rapist simply by being unable to prove she or he obtained explicit verbal consent to every sexual activity throughout a sexual encounter. How might an innocent student demonstrate he or she received affirmative consent under California's new law, for example? In response to this question, the statute's co-author, Assemblywoman Bonnie Lowenthal, simply said, "Your guess is as good as mine."

The concept of affirmative consent was first brought to national attention when it was adopted by Ohio's historic Antioch College in the early 1990s. When news of the college's policy became public in 1993, the practical difficulty of adhering to the policy prompted national ridicule so widespread that it was lampooned on *Saturday Night Live*. (Indeed, the fallout from the policy's adoption has been cited as a factor in the college's decline and eventual closing in 2007. It has since reopened.) The awkwardness of enforcing "affirmative consent" rules upon the reality of human sexual behavior has continued to be a popular subject for comedy by television shows such as *Chappelle's Show* and *New Girl*. The humor found in the profound disconnect between the policy's bureaucratic requirements for sexual interaction and human sexuality as a lived and various experience underscores the serious difficulty that affirmative consent now presents to administrators across California, New York, and other campuses nationwide.

Consent: Intoxication and Incapacitation

Because many cases of sexual misconduct involve one or more intoxicated students and questions about their ability to meaningfully consent to sexual activity, a university's definitions of "intoxication" and "incapacitation" are important when considering due process rights and fair procedures. To properly protect student autonomy and ensure just outcomes, university policies should distinguish between intoxication and incapacitation: Incapacitated students cannot consent, but intoxicated students may.

Being "incapacitated" is qualitatively different from

being "intoxicated." All alcoholic beverages are intoxicants, leaving all individuals who consume them—even a single drink—technically intoxicated. But if one is incapacitated, one has moved far beyond simple intoxication; indeed, one can no longer effectively function and thus cannot truly consent.

Courts confronting this problem have recognized that simple intoxication does not necessarily equal incapacitation and therefore does not necessarily foreclose consent. In *People v. Giardino* (2000), the California Court of Appeals wrote:

> It is not enough that the victim was intoxicated to some degree, or that the intoxication reduced the victim's sexual inhibitions. Impaired mentality may exist and yet the individual may be able to exercise reasonable judgment with respect to the particular matter presented to his or her mind. Instead, the level of intoxication and the resulting mental impairment must have been so great that the victim could no longer exercise reasonable judgment concerning that issue. [Internal citations and quotations omitted.]

Parsing consent is tough work, and the line separating "intoxication" from "incapacitation" can be difficult to ascertain. But this is a crucial boundary to establish if a college or university wants to ensure that its definition of consent for the purposes of sexual assault isn't absurdly broad. Otherwise, all students who have any kind of sexual contact with someone who has had even one drink have technically committed sexual assault.

FIRE has assisted institutions with this important distinction. For example, prior to intervention from FIRE, Duke University's 2009 Sexual Misconduct policy read:

> Conduct will be considered "without consent" if no clear consent, verbal or nonverbal, is given. It should be noted that in some situations an individual's ability to freely consent is taken away by another person or circumstance. **Examples include, but are not limited to, when an individual is intoxicated, "high,"** scared, physically or psychologically pressured or forced, passed out, intimidated, coerced, mentally or physically impaired, beaten, threatened, isolated, or confined. [Emphasis added.]

When we pointed out the problems with this broad definition, Duke changed its policy to read:

> Conduct will be considered "without consent" if no clear consent, verbal or nonverbal, is given. It should be noted that in some situations an individual's ability to freely consent is taken away by another person or circumstance. **Examples include, but are not limited to, when an individual is incapacitated due to alcohol or other drugs**, scared, physically forced, passed out, intimidated, coerced, mentally or physically impaired, beaten, threatened, isolated, or confined. [Emphasis added.]

The revised policy properly recognizes that incapacitated students cannot consent. It also recognizes that stripping adults of the ability to consent upon mere intoxication is problematic and misrepresents their agency in many circumstances.

Another possible policy fix for colleges seeking to strike the right balance between protecting students' ability to make their own choices and preventing sexual assault on campus is to adopt a policy that tracks municipal or state law. The vast majority of college students are adults, with all of the attendant legal rights and responsibilities; having a consistent definition of "incapacitation" both on and off campus may help ensure that students conform their behavior not only to campus policy but also to public statute.

The bottom line is that if colleges and universities are going to adjudicate serious charges like sexual assault, as OCR has dictated that they must under Title IX, they must do so in a way that is fair for all students and that doesn't render anyone who's had a drink an automatic victim.

Role for Law Enforcement?

FIRE strongly believes that sexual assault should be understood and addressed as the felony it is, whether it occurs on or off campus.

The status quo is untenable. A 2014 YouGov/*Huffington Post* survey found that just 14 percent of Americans believe that colleges do a "good job" of handling reports of rape, sexual assault, and sexual harassment. This distressing result is a symptom of the demonstrated inability of campus administrators to effectively and fairly adjudicate allegations of sexual assault, a failure documented by headline after headline in media outlets nationwide. There is a fundamental conflict of interest created by empowering campus administrators, whose primary loyalties lie with their institutions, to internally resolve serious criminal allegations. Campus disciplinary systems lack both the procedural safeguards necessary to protect the accused and the power necessary to properly punish those found guilty of heinous crimes.

While campus administrators are in many cases doing their best, they are neither qualified nor equipped to respond properly to sexual assault allegations. Student conduct administrators simply lack the investigative ability, impartiality, professional training, and legal knowledge required to reliably adjudicate sexual assault cases.

Colleges have a vital role to play in ensuring the well-being of their students. They should be well equipped to provide resources and counseling to students reporting sexual assault and to take necessary administrative action while criminal complaints are pending. To the extent that the criminal justice system fails sexual assault victims, changes to that system should be considered so that citizens both on and off campus can benefit.

Some proposed federal legislation, like the Campus

Accountability and Safety Act introduced in both the Senate and the House of Representatives, would require institutions to enter into agreements with local law enforcement agencies to "clearly delineate responsibilities and share information" regarding crimes like sexual assault. Mandating a formal relationship with local law enforcement is a small but necessary step towards ensuring that the expertise, experience, and resources of the criminal justice system are brought to bear on these investigations. Still, more needs to be done.

Sexual Harassment and the First Amendment

Both federal courts and the Department of Education's Office for Civil Rights consider sexual assault—like rape—to be an egregious instance of sexual harassment. In turn, sexual harassment is itself considered to be a form of discrimination based on sex, and is thus prohibited by Title IX. Under this interpretation, both sexual assault and sexual harassment implicate Title IX, so OCR requires colleges and universities to treat allegations of sexual harassment in the same way they treat allegations of sexual assault. In other words, OCR requires colleges and universities to adhere to the policy mandates discussed above—including using the preponderance of the evidence standard and allowing both sides to appeal— when adjudicating allegations of sexual harassment, just as with sexual assault.

As a practical matter, this interpretation places

harassing speech on the same continuum as felony crimes like rape. But while both actions may constitute sex-based discrimination under Title IX, the similarity ends there. Sexual assault is violent criminal behavior and often involves complex and fact-intensive allegations—challenges that colleges and universities are often unequipped to handle. Sexual harassment, on the other hand, presents freedom of expression concerns at public universities bound by the First Amendment and private universities that promise students free speech.

Because of these fundamental differences, evaluating sexual assault and sexual harassment under the same legal framework can have the unintended effect of distorting both the harm at issue and the required response for each. Accordingly, FIRE believes that universities are more likely to create fair and effective policies when they address the issue of sexual harassment separately and distinctly from the issue of sexual assault. Addressing the issues of sexual assault and sexual harassment separately would allow colleges to more carefully consider the scope of their definitions of sexual harassment while treating sexual assault with the serious attention demanded by such heinous criminal conduct. At a minimum, institutions should maintain separate evidentiary standards for each offense. Unfortunately, OCR now prohibits them from doing so.

Colleges and universities are both legally and morally obligated to address sexual harassment and sexual violence on campus. The vast majority are also legally and morally obligated to protect freedom of expression. These responsibilities need not be in tension—if colleges and universities adopt the proper definition of sexual harassment.

THE *DAVIS* STANDARD

The Supreme Court has provided a clear standard for student-on-student harassment that simultaneously prohibits harassment and protects speech. In *Davis v. Monroe County Board of Education* (1999), the Supreme Court confronted the question of when a school could be held liable in a lawsuit for damages filed by a student victim of harassment. The Court held that a grade school properly faced liability after it demonstrated "deliberate indifference" to serious, ongoing student-on-student harassment. In reaching this conclusion, the Court formulated a definition of student-on-student harassment. The Court determined that sexual harassment in the educational context is targeted, discriminatory conduct "that is so severe, pervasive, and objectively offensive, and that so undermines and detracts from the victims' educational experience, that the victim-students are effectively denied equal access to an institution's resources and opportunities."

Fifteen years later, the *Davis* standard is still the Supreme Court's sole guidance regarding student-on-student harassment, and it remains the best definition of harassment for both students and colleges. *Davis'* central benefit is its precise balance between a school's dual responsibilities to prohibit harassment that denies a student equal access to an education and to honor freedom of expression. If merely "offensive" expression constituted harassment, then a student might be punished for telling a sensitive student a joke, reading a poem aloud, or simply voicing a dissenting political opinion. Instead, *Davis* requires the harassment not only to be offensive to the complainant but also to be objectively offensive to a reasonable person. By incorporating an objective component, *Davis* ensures that campus discourse will not be limited to only that which is acceptable to the college's most sensitive student or by those feigning outrage to silence viewpoints they dislike. Furthermore, by requiring a showing of both "severity" and "pervasiveness," *Davis* safeguards the dialogue we expect universities to foster in the search for truth. Under the *Davis* standard, heated discussion is acceptable, but the truly harassing behavior that federal anti-discrimination laws are intended to prohibit is not.

2003 "DEAR COLLEAGUE" LETTER REGARDING THE FIRST AMENDMENT

In 2003, OCR issued a "Dear Colleague" letter to college and university presidents nationwide regarding the First Amendment. The 2003 letter was necessitated by a steady stream of controversies regarding the punishment of offensive, unpopular, or "politically incorrect" (but protected) speech on campus as instances of harassment. In the letter, former Assistant Secretary for Civil Rights Gerald A. Reynolds addressed confusion regarding the role of OCR regulation with regard to campus speech, noting that "some colleges and universities have interpreted OCR's prohibition of 'harassment' as encompassing all offensive speech regarding sex, disability, race or other classifications." To clarify, Reynolds wrote, "I want to assure you in the clearest possible terms that OCR's regulations are not intended to restrict the exercise of any activities protected under the U.S. Constitution." OCR's letter made clear that "OCR's regulations and policies do not require or prescribe speech, conduct or harassment codes that impair the exercise of rights protected under the First Amendment." It further noted that "OCR is committed to the full, fair and effective enforcement of these statutes *consistent with the requirements of the First Amendment.*" (Emphasis added.)

Under pressure from FIRE and other civil liberties groups, and following recent missteps, OCR recommitted itself to its 2003 "Dear Colleague" letter in 2013 and 2014.

In May 2013, the Departments of Justice and Education issued a findings letter announcing a resolution agreement with the University of Montana, ending a joint federal investigation into the university's policies and practices regarding sexual harassment and assault. The findings letter, which referred to the agreement as "a blueprint for colleges and universities throughout the country to protect students from sexual harassment and assault," explained the Departments' interpretation of applicable legal standards. The Departments defined sexual harassment as "any unwelcome conduct of a sexual nature" and made clear that "unwelcome conduct" included "verbal conduct"—in other words, speech. Worse still, this federal "blueprint" explicitly rejected use of the *Davis* standard's objectivity component, stating that "[w]hether conduct is objectively offensive ... is not the standard to determine whether conduct was 'unwelcome conduct of a sexual nature' and therefore constitutes 'sexual harassment.'" In other words, under this shockingly broad standard, speech that is offensive only to the most unreasonably sensitive person—including a vast range of speech protected by the First Amendment—constitutes sexual harassment.

Joined by allies from across the political spectrum, FIRE protested the federal "blueprint," repeatedly challenging OCR as to how this broad definition of harassment aligned with the First Amendment and with previous agency guidance like the 2003 "Dear Colleague" letter. As FIRE and others pointed out, federal courts have struck down university sexual harassment policies similar to the "blueprint" definition. In *DeJohn v. Temple University* (2008), for example, the United States Court of Appeals for the Third Circuit struck down a campus anti-harassment policy that, like the blueprint's definition, failed to require that the allegedly harassing speech be evaluated objectively.

In response to widespread outrage about the blueprint's threat to free speech on campus, OCR backed away from the broad language of the Montana agreement. Indeed, the actual policies adopted by the University of Montana itself departed from the broad definition announced by the blueprint, as have other agreements with universities entered into by OCR.

Further, in a letter to FIRE, Assistant Secretary for Civil Rights Catherine Lhamon stated that OCR's understanding of hostile environment harassment is "consistent" with the definition of sexual harassment in the educational context provided by the Supreme Court in *Davis*. Similarly, Acting Assistant Secretary for Civil Rights Seth Galanter assured FIRE that the 2003 "Dear Colleague" letter remained "fully in effect," and that OCR's enforcement of anti-discrimination laws like Title IX would not "restrict the exercise of any expressive activities or speech protected under the U.S. Constitution." Finally, in a 2014 "Frequently Asked Questions" document about universities' institutional obligations under Title IX, OCR made clear that "Title IX protects students from sex discrimination; it does not regulate the content of speech. OCR recognizes that the offensiveness of a particular expression as perceived by some students, standing alone, is not a legally sufficient basis to establish a hostile environment under Title IX. Title IX also does not require, prohibit, or abridge the use of particular textbooks or curricular materials."

VAGUE HARASSMENT CODES VIOLATE DUE
PROCESS RIGHTS

In considering the sufficiency of your institution's definition of sexual harassment or harassment more generally,
keep in mind that courts have consistently struck down
overly broad or vague harassment codes maintained by
public colleges on First Amendment grounds. In decisions dating back 25 years, courts have refused to allow
harassment policies to infringe upon student and faculty
First Amendment rights at public institutions (and, in
California, at private, non-sectarian institutions, thanks
to California's "Leonard Law"). The problems most often
presented by unconstitutional harassment policies are
detailed more fully in other FIRE publications, like our
Guide to Free Speech on Campus and *Correcting Common
Mistakes in Campus Speech Policies.* But when a harassment policy is impermissibly vague, that failing implicates due process rights, and should thus be considered
in this *Guide.*

In *Grayned v. City of Rockford* (1972), the Supreme
Court ruled that a regulation or law is unconstitutionally
vague when it fails to "give a person of ordinary intelligence a reasonable opportunity to know what is prohibited, so that he may act accordingly." A vague prohibition
means that citizens cannot readily ascertain the boundaries of acceptable conduct, and this lack of clarity violates due process by failing to provide citizens with basic
notice of what they may and may not lawfully do. With
regard to speech, vague policies create what's known as
a "chilling effect" on protected expression, as citizens

188

choose to self-censor rather than run afoul of amorphous or subjective regulations.

A harassment policy that, for example, simply prohibited "bullying" would almost certainly be void for vagueness. By failing to provide students with a clear, objective definition of "bullying," the policy forces students to guess at what an administrator may deem to be punishable. Even if students are somehow able to determine what a given administrator might regard as "bullying," they will likely make the rational choice to keep their mouths shut rather than risk punishment. This self-censorship chills campus expression. Indeed, in *Grayned*, the Court recognized that "[u]ncertain meanings inevitably lead citizens to 'steer far wider of the unlawful zone ... than if the boundaries of the forbidden areas were clearly marked.'" Again, at a public university, this lack of notice violates both your right to freedom of expression and your right to due process.

In fact, these failings are particularly problematic in the university setting, where speech is supposed to be at its most free. In *Dambrot v. Central Michigan University* (1995), the United States Court of Appeals for the Sixth Circuit struck down Central Michigan University's harassment policy, which prohibited "any intentional, unintentional, physical, verbal, or nonverbal behavior that subjects an individual to an intimidating, hostile or offensive educational, employment or living environment." Citing an earlier opinion, the Sixth Circuit noted:

> Vagueness may take two forms, both of which result in a denial of due process. A vague

ordinance denies fair notice of the standard of conduct to which a citizen is held accountable. At the same time an ordinance is void for vagueness if it is an unrestricted delegation of power, which in practice leaves the definition of its terms to law enforcement officers, and thereby invites arbitrary, discriminatory and overzealous enforcement.

Applying this framework to Central Michigan's policy, the Sixth Circuit found that the policy failed on both fronts. First, the court noted that to determine whether speech was "offensive" under the policy, would-be student speakers would have to make a subjective assessment, because "different people find different things offensive." Therefore, because offensiveness is subjective, the court found that the policy did "not provide fair notice of what speech will violate the policy"—and thus violated student due process rights. Second, the policy gave Central Michigan administrators sole power to define what is and is not sufficiently offensive to earn punishment. The Sixth Circuit concluded that this constituted precisely the "unrestricted delegation of power" that "invites arbitrary, discriminatory and overzealous enforcement," again violating due process. After review, the Sixth Circuit struck down Central Michigan's harassment policy.

Review your university's harassment policy to ensure that it doesn't suffer from the same fatal flaws. If it does, suggest to your administrator that adopting the *Davis* standard would simultaneously prohibit discriminatory harassment while respecting student rights to free expression and due process. Again, these twin legal and moral obligations borne by universities need not be in tension.

WHAT TO EXPECT WHEN YOU'RE ACCUSED OF...

Regardless of the charges you face, your best defense is to be prepared. Research your school's policies and procedures so you know precisely how your institution defines the offense you've been accused of committing and the promises your school has made you regarding due process protections like notice, a hearing, and a right to appeal. If your college's policies guarantee you a right, be sure to demand it be provided. Your knowledge of the institutional policies governing your situation may prove to be the difference between a just outcome and a denial of due process.

With this general advice in mind, certain charges may involve particular considerations that you should keep in mind. **Please note that the scenarios discussed below are intended for students at public colleges, although arguments about basic fairness may prove persuasive at private colleges as well.** And again, the following is not intended as formal legal advice. If you seek legal advice, contact an attorney.

Poor Academic Performance

If you face suspension or expulsion for academic reasons, like poor grades, your expectations for due process protections should be low.

Courts have consistently deferred to colleges and universities to make academic decisions for themselves without judicial oversight, believing educators to be far better suited than judges to do so. In actions concerning academic misconduct, you are likely entitled to notice of your institution's concerns prior to any adverse action against you, so that you might have a chance to correct the problems. You likely will not be afforded a hearing, however, as courts have declined to require one in these situations. Above all, you should make sure that the final decision to suspend or expel you has been made in a careful, deliberate way—in other words, that your college or university had well-documented, substantial reasons to punish you. Relatedly, if you have solid evidence suggesting that your college is using your academic performance as a pretext for punishing you for other behavior—your campus activism, for example—then you should present that evidence to school administrators as soon as possible.

Plagiarism and Cheating

If you face punishment for plagiarism or cheating, you may expect more substantial due process protections than you might if you faced punishment simply for poor academic performance. Determining the validity of plagiarism or cheating accusations involves a degree of fact-finding—that is, figuring out what actually happened—so it is not a purely academic question and need not be left solely to educators.

You should expect and can demand to receive notice of the charge against you. Ideally, this notice should be both timely (allowing you sufficient time to prepare your defense) and thorough (providing you with full knowledge of the evidence supporting the charges against you). If it isn't, you should protest this deficiency in writing, documenting the flawed notice and explaining how it negatively impacted your ability to defend yourself. Send the college administrators a copy of your concerns, and be sure to save a copy for yourself. It may prove useful in a later appeal or court challenge.

You should expect and can demand some kind of hearing in which you can tell your side of the story, rebut the allegations against you, and challenge the accounts of opposing witnesses. You should be allowed to present any exculpatory witnesses or evidence you may have. The hearing panel must be impartial and you must be presumed innocent until proven guilty by at least a preponderance of the evidence. Again, if you are denied any or all of these rights, you should protest this failing with a written letter detailing the flaws and explaining how these failings denied you a fair hearing.

If the hearing panel decides against you, you should ask for written findings of fact explaining the reasoning for the decision. Be sure to review your college's procedures to determine if you have a right to appeal and, if so, on what grounds.

Drug Possession and Other Non-Violent Criminal Conduct

If you face punishment for drug possession or other non-violent criminal conduct, you should expect substantial due process protections. Because you face a purely disciplinary charge with serious consequences for a guilty finding, you are entitled to demand more substantial due process protections.

Because the misconduct of which you are accused violates not only campus policy but also criminal law, you may be facing criminal charges, as well. Accordingly, you should retain an attorney to advise you. Your attorney should ask the college to delay its proceedings until any criminal justice proceedings are concluded. If the college refuses, you and your attorney should discuss precisely if and how you will answer questions in the college hearing, as your testimony there could be used against you in any concurrent criminal proceedings concerning the same alleged misconduct.

You should expect and can demand to receive notice of the charges against you. Ideally, this notice should be both timely (allowing you sufficient time to prepare your defense) and thorough (providing you with full knowledge of the evidence supporting the charges against you).

If it isn't, you should protest this deficiency in writing, documenting the flawed notice and explaining how it negatively impacted your ability to defend yourself. Send the college administrators a copy of your concerns, and be sure to save a copy for yourself. It may prove useful in a later appeal or court challenge.

You should expect and can demand some kind of hearing in which you can tell your side of the story, rebut the allegations against you, and challenge the accounts of opposing witnesses. You should be allowed to present any exculpatory witnesses or evidence you may have. The hearing panel must be impartial and you must be presumed innocent until proven guilty. Given the seriousness of the charge, the standard of proof by which the university must prove you guilty *should* require at least clear and convincing evidence of your misconduct. In practice, it may not. But again, if you are denied any or all of these rights, you should protest this failing with a written letter detailing the flaws and explaining how these failings denied you a fair hearing.

If the hearing panel decides against you, you should ask for written findings of fact explaining the reasoning for the decision. Be sure to review your college's procedures to determine if you have a right to appeal and, if so, on what grounds.

Speech-Related Misconduct

If you face punishment for speech-related misconduct, such as "offensive" or harassing speech, your First

Amendment rights (or, at a private university, the free speech rights promised to you by your institution) are implicated by both your university's policy and any investigation or punishment you face as a result of your expression. Because you face a purely disciplinary charge that involves expressive activity, your first consideration should be to determine the constitutionality of the policy you are charged with violating. (If you attend a private institution that promises free speech, the fact that a policy would be unconstitutional off campus is a good indication that it also violates your school's promises.) If your college or university's policy is overly broad (*i.e.*, prohibits speech protected by the First Amendment) or vague (*i.e.*, fails to provide sufficient notice as to what speech is prohibited), then enforcement of it violates your First Amendment rights. Likewise, if the speech at issue is protected by the First Amendment, then any extended investigation or punishment of it violates your First Amendment rights.

To determine whether your speech is protected or your university's policy passes constitutional muster, refer to FIRE's *Guide to Free Speech on Campus*, available free of charge on FIRE's website (thefire.org). You should also visit FIRE's Spotlight database (thefire.org/spotlight), which catalogs the speech codes maintained by over 400 colleges and universities, to see if we've evaluated your institution's policies. Of course, if you have any questions or believe you are facing investigation and punishment due to protected expression, you should contact FIRE immediately.

Sexual Harassment and Sexual Assault

If you face punishment for sexual assault, you should expect and demand substantial due process protections. Because you face a purely disciplinary charge with serious consequences for a guilty finding, you should be entitled to substantial due process protections. Unfortunately, because of the legislative and administrative activity in this area, detailed in Part V, your rights have been eroded.

Because the misconduct of which you are accused violates not only campus policy but also criminal law, you may be facing criminal charges, as well. Accordingly, you should retain an attorney to advise you as soon as possible. Unfortunately, per Office for Civil Rights guidance, your university will likely refuse to delay the proceedings against you while the criminal case against you continues.

You should expect and can demand to receive notice of the charge against you. Ideally, this notice should be both timely (allowing you sufficient time to prepare your defense) and thorough (providing you with full knowledge of the evidence supporting the charges against you). If it isn't, you should protest this deficiency in writing, documenting the flawed notice and explaining how it negatively impacted your ability to defend yourself. Send the college administrators a copy of your concerns, and be sure to save a copy for yourself. It may prove useful in a later appeal or court challenge.

You should expect and can demand some kind of

hearing in which you can tell your side of the story, rebut the allegations against you, and challenge the accounts of opposing witnesses. Per the Violence Against Women Act Reauthorization, you are entitled to be accompanied by your attorney to all meetings and hearings regarding the charge or charges against you.

Unfortunately, due to OCR guidance, you will likely be unable to directly cross-examine your accuser and opposing witnesses. You should ask to pose questions to them via a panel or administrator, instead. You should be allowed to present any exculpatory witnesses or evidence you may have. The hearing panel must be impartial and you must be presumed innocent until proven guilty. Despite the seriousness of the charge, you will likely be tried under the low "preponderance of the evidence" standard of proof due to OCR guidance.

If the hearing panel decides against you, you should ask for written findings of fact explaining the reasoning for the decision. Be sure to review your college's procedures to determine if you have a right to appeal and, if so, on what grounds. If you are afforded the right to appeal a ruling, bear in mind that per OCR guidance, your accuser may appeal, as well.

CONCLUSION

Forewarned is forearmed.

If you are accused of wrongdoing, you enjoy fewer procedural protections on campus than you would off campus. There are limits, however, to the authority of college and university administrators over you. This is especially true at public colleges and universities, though private college students are not without recourse.

This *Guide* has sought to inform you of your legal rights. It has also endeavored to teach you the moral arguments for the procedural and substantive safeguards that individuals in a free and decent society should expect to receive. This *Guide* has explained to you the means at your disposal to defend yourself, your honor, and your rights.

If you have to use this *Guide*, we hope that it increases the fairness with which you are treated and the likelihood of a just result. We hope that it aids you in establishing the truth.

A caveat: This *Guide* is just that—a guide. It is not

meant as a substitute for legal advice and representation. If you get into trouble, there is no substitute for the guidance of a legal professional. FIRE hopes that this *Guide* will prove valuable to students as well as to legal professionals.

We also hope that many readers have no need of this *Guide* to protect themselves. If you are in that fortunate category, please use this *Guide* to make your campus one that offers the civilized procedures and protections that you would wish for yourself, your friends, and your loved ones. Justice is an immeasurably precious thing, and due process is an essential part of justice.

APPENDIX: THE FIRST, FIFTH, AND FOURTEENTH AMENDMENTS

Amendment I

Congress shall make no law respecting an establishment of religion, or prohibiting the free exercise thereof; or abridging the freedom of speech, or of the press; or the right of the people peaceably to assemble, and to petition the government for a redress of grievances.

Amendment V

No person shall be held to answer for a capital, or otherwise infamous crime, unless on a presentment or indictment of a grand jury, except in cases arising in the land or naval forces, or in the militia, when in actual service in time of war or public danger; nor shall any person be subject for the same offence to be twice put in jeopardy of life or limb; nor shall be compelled in any criminal case to be a witness against himself, nor be deprived of life, liberty, or property, without due process of law; nor shall private property be taken for public use without just compensation.

Amendment XIV

Section 1. All persons born or naturalized in the United States, and subject to the jurisdiction thereof, are citizens of the United States and of the state wherein they reside. No state shall make or enforce any law which shall abridge the privileges or immunities of citizens of the United States; nor shall any state deprive any person of life, liberty, or property, without due process of law; nor deny to any person within its jurisdiction the equal protection of the laws.

CASE APPENDIX

The following cases were discussed in the text of the *Guide*. Their legal citations are below.

Addington v. Texas, 441 U.S. 418 (1979)

Babcock v. New Orleans Baptist Theological Seminary, 554 So. 2d 90 (La. App. 4 Cir. 1989)

Barnes v. Zaccari, 669 F.3d 1295 (11th Cir. 2012)

Baxter v. Palmigiano, 425 U.S. 308 (1976)

Board of Curators of the University of Missouri v. Horowitz, 435 U.S. 78 (1978)

California v. Green, 399 U.S. 149 (1970)

Carr v. St. John's University, 231 N.Y.S.2d 410 (App. Div. 1962)

Corso v. Creighton University, 731 F.2d 529 (8th Cir. 1984)

Dambrot v. Central Michigan University, 55 F.3d 1177 (6th Cir. 1995)

Davis v. Monroe County Board of Education, 526 U.S. 629 (1999)

DeJohn v. Temple University, 537 F.3d 301 (3d Cir. 2008)

Dixon v. Alabama State Board of Education, 294 F.2d 150 (5th Cir. 1961)

Donohue v. Baker, 976 F. Supp. 136 (N.D.N.Y. 1997)

Fellheimer v. Middlebury College, 869 F. Supp. 238 (D. Vt. 1994)

Case Appendix

Flaim v. Medical College of Ohio, 418 F.3d 629 (6th Cir. 2005)

French v. Bashful, 303 F. Supp. 1333 (E.D. La. 1969)

Furey v. Temple University, 730 F. Supp. 2d 380 (E.D. Pa. 2010)

Furey v. Temple University, 884 F. Supp. 2d 223 (E.D. Pa. 2012)

Furutani v. Ewigleben, 297 F. Supp. 1163 (N.D. Cal. 1969)

Gabrilowitz v. Newman, 582 F.2d 100 (1st Cir. 1978)

Garrity v. New Jersey, 385 U.S. 493 (1967)

Giles v. Howard University, 428 F. Supp. 603 (D.C. 1977)

Goldberg v. Regents of the University of California, 248 Cal. App. 2d 867 (Ct. App. 1967)

Gomes v. University of Maine System, 365 F. Supp. 2d 6 (D. Me. 2005)

Gonzaga University v. Doe, 536 U.S. 273 (2002)

Goodreau v. Rector & Visitors of University of Virginia, 116 F. Supp. 2d 694 (W.D. Va. 2000)

Gorman v. University of Rhode Island, 837 F.2d 7 (1st Cir. 1988)

Goss v. Lopez, 419 U.S. 565 (1975)

Grayned v. City of Rockford, 408 U.S. 104 (1972)

Hardison v. Florida Agricultural & Mechanical University, 706 So. 2d 111 (Fla. 1998)

Harwood v. Johns Hopkins University, 747 A.2d 205 (Md. Ct. Spec. App. 2000)

Healy v. James, 408 U.S. 169 (1972)

Jaber v. Wayne State University Board of Governors, 788 F. Supp. 2d 572 (E.D. Mich. 2011)

Jaksa v. Regents of University of Michigan, 597 F. Supp. 1245 (E.D. Mich. 1984)

Kickertz v. New York University, 952 N.Y.S.2d 147 (App. Div. 2012)

King v. DePauw University, 2014 WL 4197507 (S.D. Ind. Aug. 22, 2014)

Lee v. Macon County Board of Education, 490 F.2d 458 (5th Cir. 1974)

Case Appendix

Marshall v. Maguire, 102 Misc. 2d 697 (N.Y. Sup. Ct. 1980)

Mathews v. Eldridge, 424 U.S. 319 (1976)

McDonald v. Board of Trustees of the University of Illinois, 375 F. Supp. 95 (N.D. Ill. 1974)

Morale v. Grigel, 422 F. Supp. 988 (D.N.H. 1976)

Morrison v. University of Oregon Health Science Center, 68 Ore. App. 870 (1984)

Nash v. Auburn University, 812 F.2d 655 (11th Cir. 1987)

Paine v. Board of Regents of University of Texas System, 355 F. Supp. 199 (W.D. Tex 1972)

People v. Giardino, 98 Cal. Rptr. 2d 315 (Ct. App. 2000)

Ray v. Wilmington College, 667 N.E.2d 39 (Ohio Ct. App. 1995)

Regents of University of Michigan v. Ewing, 474 U.S. 214 (1985)

Reichenberg v. Nelson, 310 F. Supp. 248 (D. Neb. 1970)

Schaer v. Brandeis, 432 Mass. 474 (2000)

Sill v. Pennsylvania State University, 462 F.2d 463 (3d Cir. 1973)

Soglin v. Kauffman, 418 F.2d 163 (7th Cir. 1969)

Soper v. Hoben, 195 F.3d 845 (6th Cir. 1999)

State of New Jersey v. Schmid, 84 N.J. 535 (1980)

Tedeschi v. Wagner College, 49 N.Y.2d 652 (N.Y. 1980)

Texas Medical School v. Than, 901 S.W.2d 926 (Tex. 1995)

United States v. Miami University, 294 F.3d 797 (6th Cir. 2002)

Vaksman v. Alcorn, 877 S.W. 2d 390 (Tex. Ct. App. 1994)

Waliga v. Board of Trustees of Kent State University, 488 N.E.2d 850 (Ohio 1986)

Woodis v. Westark, 160 F.3d 435 (8th Cir. 1998)

Progression of Campus Disciplinary Process

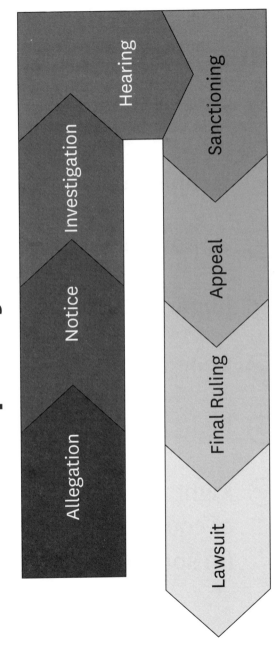

Checklist of Basic Rights

- ✓ Presumption of innocence

- ✓ Meaningful written notice

- ✓ Opportunity to be heard

- ✓ Impartial tribunal

- ✓ Right to confront accuser

- ✓ Right to record hearing

- ✓ Right to active participation of counsel/advisor (in some states)

It's Time To Consider Hiring a Lawyer When...

... the alleged misconduct could result in a criminal charge.

... the punishment would be life-altering.

... the charges are unclear or keep changing.

... you aren't told exactly what actions or incident led to the charges.

... administrators aren't listening to you.

... campus politics appear to be dictating the outcome of your case.

... your case is in the media.

... you are suffering adverse consequences for proclaiming your innocence.

10 Tips for Ensuring Justice

1. Be prepared! Read your student handbook carefully.
2. Insist on timely, meaningful notice.
3. Research similar charges for comparable outcomes.
4. Inspect all records.
5. Confirm all conversations with administrators in writing.
6. Take advantage of your opportunity to tell your side of the story.
7. Question accusers and witnesses.
8. Record your hearing and/or obtain transcript.
9. Appeal if necessary.
10. Talk to others: FIRE, an advisor, an attorney, or the press.

5 Core Arguments for Due Process

1. Due process is an essential civil liberty and a prerequisite for life in a democratic society.

2. Due process is a necessary check against human fallibility.

3. Due process results in trustworthy verdicts, which benefit the accuser, the accused, and the whole campus community.

4. Many of the most important due process protections cost the university nothing.

5. While university hearings aren't criminal hearings, the stakes can nevertheless be very high, rendering serious due process protections crucially important.

FIRE'S *GUIDES* TO
STUDENT RIGHTS ON CAMPUS
BOARD OF EDITORS

Vivian Berger - Vivian Berger is the Nash Professor of Law Emerita at Columbia Law School. Berger is a former New York County Assistant District Attorney and a former Assistant Counsel to the NAACP Legal Defense and Educational Fund. She has done significant work in the fields of criminal law and procedure (in particular, the death penalty and habeas corpus) and mediation, and continues to use her expertise in various settings, both public and private. Berger is General Counsel for and a National Board Member of the American Civil Liberties Union and has written numerous essays and journal articles on human rights and due process. She is a regular columnist for the *National Law Journal.*

212

Today. He is also past National President of the Society of Professional Journalists and former executive director of the First Amendment Center at Vanderbilt University.

Edwin Meese III - Edwin Meese III holds the Ronald Reagan Chair in Public Policy at the Heritage Foundation. He is also Chairman of Heritage's Center for Legal and Judicial Studies. Meese is a Distinguished Visiting Fellow at the Hoover Institution at Stanford University, and a Distinguished Senior Fellow at The University of London's Institute of United States Studies. He has also served as Chairman of the governing board at George Mason University in Virginia and was the 75th Attorney General of the United States in the Reagan administration.

Roger Pilon - Roger Pilon is Vice President for Legal Affairs at the Cato Institute, where he holds the B. Kenneth Simon Chair in Constitutional Studies, directs Cato's Center for Constitutional Studies, and publishes the *Cato Supreme Court Review*. Prior to joining Cato, he held five senior posts in the Reagan administration. He has taught philosophy and law, and was a National Fellow at Stanford's Hoover Institution. Pilon has published widely in moral, political, and legal theory and serves as an adjunct professor of government at Georgetown University.

Jamin Raskin - Jamin Raskin is Professor of Law at American University Washington College of Law, specializing in constitutional law and the First Amendment, and Director of WCL's Program on Law and Government and founder of the Marshall-Brennan Constitutional Literacy Project, which sends law students into public high schools to teach the Constitution. He served as a member of the Clinton-Gore Justice Department Transition Team, as Assistant Attorney General in the Commonwealth of Massachusetts, and as General Counsel for the National Rainbow Coalition. He currently serves as a State Senator in Maryland. Raskin has also been a Teaching Fellow in the Government Department at Harvard University and has won several awards for his scholarly essays and journal articles. He is author of *We the Students* among other books and publications.

Nadine Strossen - Nadine Strossen is the former President of the American Civil Liberties Union, a member of its National Advisory Council, and Professor of Law at New York Law School. Strossen has published approximately 250 works in scholarly and general interest publications, and is author of two significant books on the importance of civil liberties to the struggle for equality. She has lectured and practiced extensively in the areas of constitutional law and civil liberties, and is a frequent commentator in the national media on various legal issues.

ABOUT FIRE

FIRE's mission is to defend and sustain individual rights at America's colleges and universities. These rights include freedom of speech, legal equality, due process, religious liberty, and sanctity of conscience—the essential qualities of individual liberty and dignity. FIRE's core mission is to protect the unprotected and to educate the public and communities of concerned Americans about the threats to these rights on our campuses and about the means to preserve them.

FIRE is a nonpartisan charitable and educational tax-exempt foundation within the meaning of Section 501(c)(3) of the Internal Revenue Code. Contributions to FIRE are deductible to the fullest extent provided by tax laws. FIRE does not receive government funding. Please visit **thefire.org** for more information about FIRE.

FIRE'S *GUIDES* TO STUDENT RIGHTS ON CAMPUS

FIRE believes it imperative that our nation's future leaders be educated as members of a free society. Toward that end, FIRE implemented its path-breaking series of *Guides* to Student Rights on Campus.

The creation and distribution of these *Guides* is indispensable to challenging and ending the climate of censorship and enforced self-censorship on our college campuses. This climate profoundly threatens the future of this nation's full enjoyment of and preservation of liberty.

A distinguished group of legal scholars serves as Board of Editors to this series. The board, selected from across the political and ideological spectrum, has advised FIRE on each of the *Guides*. The diversity of this board proves that liberty on campus is not a question of partisan politics, but of the rights and responsibilities of free individuals in a society governed by the rule of law.

It is our liberty, above all else, that defines us as human beings, capable of reason, ethics, and responsibility. The struggle for liberty on American campuses is one of the defining struggles of our age. A nation that does not educate in freedom will not survive in freedom and will not even know when freedom has been lost.

Individuals too often convince themselves that they are caught up in moments of history that they cannot affect. That history, however, is made by their will and moral choices. There is a moral crisis in higher education. It will not be resolved unless we choose and act to resolve it. We invite you to join our fight.

Please visit thefire.org/guides for more information on FIRE's *Guides* to Student Rights on Campus. Students interested in working with FIRE to defend civil liberties on campus should join the FIRE Student Network by visiting thefire.org/student-network.

CONTACTING FIRE
thefire.org

Send inquiries, comments, and documented instances of violations of free speech, individual liberty, religious freedom, and the rights of conscience, legal equality, due process, and academic freedom on campus via one of the methods below:

Case submissions via website only.

By Email:
fire@thefire.org

By Mail:
Foundation for Individual Rights in Education
170 S. Independence Mall W., Suite 510
Philadelphia, Pennsylvania 19106

By Phone or Fax:
Phone: 215-717-FIRE (3473)
Fax: 215-717-3440

Submit a Case:
www.thefire.org/cases/submit

AUTHORS

Harvey A. Silverglate

Josh Gewolb

EDITOR

William Creeley

Harvey A. Silverglate, Co-founder and Chairman of the Board of Directors of the Foundation for Individual Rights in Education, is a lawyer, journalist, lecturer, and writer who for 47 years has specialized in civil liberties and criminal defense work. He is the co-author, with Alan Charles Kors, of *The Shadow University: The Betrayal of Liberty on America's Campuses.*

Josh Gewolb is an attorney in private practice in Rochester, New York. He is a graduate of Harvard College and the University of Michigan Law School.

William Creeley is Vice President of Legal and Public Advocacy for the Foundation for Individual Rights in Education. A graduate of New York University School of Law, he has co-authored *amicus curiae* briefs submitted to the Supreme Court of the United States and the United States Courts of Appeals for the Third, Eighth, Ninth, and Eleventh Circuits. He is a member of the New York State Bar and the First Amendment Lawyers Association.

The editor thanks Frank Bellamy, Laura Beltz, Ari Cohn, Joe Cohn, David Deerson, Adam Goldstein, Samantha Harris, Andrew Kloster, Susan Kruth, Greg Lukianoff, Gina Luttrell, Azhar Majeed, Molly Nocheck, Catherine Sevcenko, and Robert Shibley for their valuable contributions to this revised Guide.

221